JOHN PAUL II IN MEXICO

JOHN PAUL II IN MEXICO

His Collected Speeches

COLLINS

Published by Collins
London   Glasgow   Cleveland   New York
Toronto   Sydney   Auckland   Johannesburg

First published in Great Britain 1979

UK ISBN 0 00 215381 5

First published in the USA 1979
Library of Congress Catalog Card Number 79–64495
USA ISBN 0–529–05682–8

Made and printed in Italy by Marietti Editori,

A Pilgrimage of Faith

Thursday 25 January

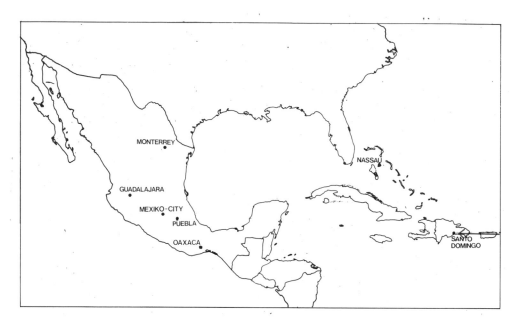

AT ROME AIRPORT

The long journey of Pope John Paul II to Latin America for the Third Conference of the Latin American Bishops was about to begin. To all the people, who had thronged to Rome Airport to say goodbye and wish the Holy Father a successful outcome of his first apostolic voyage, the Pope spoke as follows:

With all my heart I express to you my sincere thanks for your presence in this place, at the moment when, for some days, I am leaving my beloved diocese and Italy to go to Latin America.

This gesture of yours, so delicate and thoughtful, gives me comfort and is a serene augury for the success of the journey, which — as you know — wishes to be first and foremost a *pilgrimage of faith*. The Pope is going to kneel before the marvellous image of the Madonna of Guadalupe, in Mexico, to invoke her motherly assistance and her protection on his pontifical service; to say to her again, with a force increased by his immense new tasks: 'Totus tuus sum Ego!', and to put in her hands the future of evangelization in Latin America.

The Pope, furthermore, is going to other areas of the New World as a *Messenger of the Gospel* for the millions of brothers and sisters who believe in Christ. He wants to know them, embrace them and tell them all — children, young people, men, women, workers, peasants, professionals — that God loves them, that the Church loves them, that the Pope loves them, and also he wants to receive from them the encouragement and example of their goodness, their faith. Ideally, therefore, the Pope follows in the wake of the missionaries, the priests, all those who, from the discovery of the New World, spread the message of Jesus with sacrifice, abnegation and generosity in those immense lands, preaching love and peace among men.

The Pope, finally, is carrying out this journey to take part, together with his brother bishops, in the Third General Conference of the Latin American Episcopate which will take place in Puebla. The Conference will deal with important problems concerning the pastoral action of the People of God, which, in the light of the Second Vatican Council, must keep in mind the complex local socio-political situations in order to instil in them the fruitful ferments of the proclamation of the Gospel. The Pope will go to Puebla to help, to 'strengthen' (cf. Lk. 22:32) his brother bishops.

As I am preparing to undertake the flight, after greeting the Cardinal Secretary of State and the other cardinals who are here with him, I express my grateful appreciation to the Prime Minister of the Italian Government and to the civil and military authorities; I greet the Doyen of the Diplomatic Corps to the Holy See and the Ambassadors of Latin America, and all those who have come to wish me a good journey. I willingly bless you all.

ON THE AIRCRAFT

The first stage of the Pope's journey to Mexico was marked by a lengthy meeting with journalists in the section of the aircraft reserved for the press. Only a few minutes after take-off, the Pope unexpectedly walked into the press compartment and shook hands with all the journalists as he gave interviews or answered their questions in various languages with complete frankness.

The meeting lasted more than one hour, from 8.30 to 9.40 a.m. It was much the same situation as at the first audience with the press during the early days of the pontificate. John Paul II spoke of his journey and the hopes he had built upon it, and he emphasized the importance of the Vicar of Christ being present wherever men have to endure a condition of poverty and alienation and are trying to create a better future.

The Pope reminded his hearers that the main purpose of his mission was to proclaim the Gospel and bring Christ to the human race which yearned for Him—'I am making a pilgrimage of Faith', said the Pope, 'a voyage of Hope'.

In reply to certain topical questions, the Pope touched on important subjects such as the theology of liberation, violence, terrorism and the situation in Italy. Of the first, he said that it was a social programme and therefore not theology but rather sociology. Apart from this, there was nothing novel about it. It had existed as long as men had been Christian. Of terrorism, the Pope said that its cruel and bloody activities degraded European and Italian civilization. It was all the more disturbing in that those responsible for these acts remained unknown. 'We are obliged to protect ourselves', said the Pope, 'though not in order to persecute anyone.' And he added, 'We all have to protect ourselves. Even I, when I go visiting a parish, have to be accompanied by a number of policemen. My God, and why?'

As the plane flew over Turin, a journalist from one of that city's newspapers asked the Pope to address a few words to the Italian workers. 'I believe', remarked John Paul II, 'that the physical work which I did as a youngster was at least as important for me as my intellectual training.' In answer to a question about the contribution which the Church can make to Italian society, the Pope replied that, after only a hundred days of exercising his pontificate he was not yet in a position to express an opinion on Italy, but he thought, nevertheless, that the Church, whether in Italy, Mexico, Poland or elsewhere, 'is a reality which lives within a reality, and, if it will only be itself, it cannot but serve mankind and help to promote solidarity among men'. At the end of his meeting with the press,

the Pope returned to his compartment where he spent the remainder of the trip at his writing desk with his closest collaborators, putting the finishing touches to the programme of his first day of pilgrimage. Before the aircraft touched down at Santo Domingo, the Pope sent a message to the President of the USA. Then he received the members of the plane's crew expressing his thanks and good wishes to each.

THE ARRIVAL AT THE AIRPORT OF SANTO DOMINGO

The white, yellow and green aeroplane, adorned with the papal coat-of-arms, landed at Santo Domingo Airport at 1.30 p.m. local time. On leaving the aircraft, the Pope prostrated himself and kissed the soil of Latin America. With this gesture he emphasized the universality of the Church, for which no land is alien, and, in continuation of the apostolate of the first missionaries, he confirmed the love which the Church feels for the people of the American continent. After receiving the homage of the President of the Dominican Republic and of Cardinals Beras, Cooke, Baum and Medeiros, as well as that of numerous bishops and the members of the government, the Pope made the following speech:

Mr President, Brothers in the Episcopate, Brothers and Sisters,

I thank God for allowing me to arrive at this piece of American land, the beloved land of Columbus, in the first stage of my visit to a continent to which my thought has so often flown, full of esteem and trust, particularly in this initial period of my ministry as Supreme Pastor of the Church.

The aspiration of the past becomes reality with this meeting, in which so many sons of this dear Dominican land participate – and so many others will have desired to do so – with enthusiastic affection. On its behalf and on your own, Mr President, you have wished to bid me a cordial welcome with significant and noble words. I respond to them with sentiments of sincere appreciation and deep gratitude, a sign of the Pope's love for the sons of this hospitable nation.

But in the words I have listened to and in the joyful welcome that the Dominican people gives me today, I also hear the voice, distant but present, of so many other sons of all the countries of Latin America, who, from the lands of Mexico to the extreme south of the continent, feel united with the Pope by extraordinary ties which touch the depths of their being as men and as Christians. Let one and all of these countries and their sons, receive the most cordial greeting, the homage of respect and affection of the Pope, his admiration and appreciation for the stupendous values of history and of culture which they preserve, the desire for an individual, family, and community life of increasing human prosperity, in a social climate of morality, justice for all, and intense cultivation of spiritual goods.

An event of very great ecclesial importance brings me to these lands. I arrive in a continent in which the Church has left deep traces, which penetrate deep down in the history and character of each people. I come to this living portion of the Church, the most numerous one, a vital part for the future of the Catholic Church, which amid fine achievements but not without shadows, amid difficulties and sacrifices, bears witness to Christ. And today it desires to answer the challenge of the present moment, by proposing a light of hope for this life and for the next one, through its work of proclaiming the Good News which is summed up in Christ the Saviour, the Son of God and the elder Brother of men.

The Pope wishes to be close to this evangelizing Church in order to encourage its effort, to bring it new hope in its hope, to help it to discern its paths better, developing or changing what is necessary in order that it may be more and more faithful to its mission: that received from Jesus, that of Peter and his successors, that of the Apostles and of those who succeed them.

And since the Pope's visit wishes to be an enterprise of evangelization, I desired to arrive here by the route which, when the Continent was discovered, was followed by the first evangelizers: those religious who came to proclaim Christ the Saviour, to defend the dignity of the natives, to proclaim their inviolable rights, to promote their complete advancement, to teach brotherhood as men and as of the same Lord and Father, God.

This is a testimony of gratitude which I wish to render to the architects of that admirable action of evangelization, in this very land the New World in which the first cross was planted, the first Mass was celebrated, the first Hail Mary was recited and from which, amid various vicissitudes, the faith spread to other nearby islands and from there to the mainland.

From this inspiring place in the Continent, a land of fervent love for the Blessed Virgin and of uninterrupted devotion to Peter's Successor, the Pope wishes to reserve his dearest memory and greeting for the poor, the peasants, the sick and the underprivileged, who feel close to the Church, who love her, who follow Christ even in the midst of obstacles, and who, with an admirable sense of humanity, put into practice that solidarity, hospitality, honest and hopeful gaiety, for which God is preparing his reward.

Thinking of the greater good of these kind and generous peoples, I trust that those in charge, the Catholics and men of good will of the Dominican Republic and of the whole of Latin America, will commit their best energies and expand the frontiers of their creativity to build up a more human and, at the same time, a more Christian world. This is the call that the Pope makes to you at this first meeting in your land.

THE CEREMONY IN THE CATHEDRAL OF SANTO DOMINGO

From the airport to the Cathedral, along a route of 28 kilometres, the Pope was acclaimed by vast and enthusiastic crowds. At 3.45 p.m. the first meeting took place near the entrance of the Cathedral, between Pope John Paul II and the bishops, clergy, religious and representatives of all branches of the Church in the Dominican Republic. After introducing the bishops, Cardinal Octavio Antonio Beras Rojas addressed a message of homage and welcome to the Holy Father to which John Paul II replied as follows:

Lord Cardinal, Brothers in the Episcopate, Beloved Sons,

It is but a few moments since I had the happiness to arrive in your country, and now I feel a new joy on meeting you in this cathedral, dedicated to the Annunciation, where so many of you have desired to come to see the Pope: the primatial cathedral, which stands beside what was the first archiepiscopal see in America.

My thanks go in the first place to you, Lord Cardinal, for your kind words; they have filled my spirit with satisfaction, admiration and hope.

I wish to tell you that the Pope, too, desires to be with you, in order to know you and love you even more. My only regret is not to be able to meet and speak with each one of you.

But although that is not possible, rest assured that no one is excluded from the affection, from the memory, of the common father who, even though far away, thinks of you and prays for your intentions.

In order that this meeting may be more intimate, let us pray for a moment and ask the Lord, through the intercession of Our Lady of High Grace, whose image is present here, to grant that you may always be good children of the Church, that you may grow in the faith, and that yours may be a life worthy of Christians.

I very willingly impart my Blessing to you, to your fellow countrymen and members of your families, and, above all, to the sick and to those who are suffering.

And you, too, pray for the Pope.

THE CONCELEBRATION OF MASS
IN THE PLAZA DE LA INDEPENDENCIA

On entering the Cathedral, the Holy
Father went to the Chapel of the Blessed
Sacrament to pray. Then, at 5 p.m. he
conducted a concelebration of the Mass
with the Dominican bishops. Around the
altar, which had been erected in the Plaza
de la Independencia, there was a crowd
of faithful, estimated at thirty thousand
people, which included the President and
leading authorities of the Republic. After
the Gospel, the Pope preached a sermon:

Brothers in the Episcopate, Beloved Sons:

1. In this Eucharist in which we share the same faith in Christ, the Bishop
of Rome and of the universal Church, present among you, gives you his
greeting of peace: 'Grace to you and peace from God the Father and our
Lord Jesus Christ.' (Gal. 1:3.)

I come to these American lands as a pilgrim of peace and hope, to take
part in an ecclesial event of evangelization, urged in my turn by the words
of the Apostle Paul: 'If I preach the gospel, that gives me no ground for
boasting. For necessity is laid upon me. Woe to me if I do not preach the
gospel!' (1 Cor. 9:16.)

The present period of the history of humanity calls for a renewed
transmission of faith, to communicate to modern man the perennial
message of Christ, adapted to his concrete conditions of life.

This evangelization is a constant and an essential exigency of ecclesial
dynamics. In his encyclical *Evangelii Nuntiandi,* Paul VI affirmed:
'Evangelizing is in fact the grace and vocation proper to the Church, her
deepest identity. She exists in order to evangelize . . .' (n. 14.)

And the same Pontiff states that 'as an evangelizer, Christ first of all
proclaims a kingdom, the kingdom of God'. 'As the kernel and centre of
his Good News, Christ proclaims salvation, this great gift which is, above
all, liberation from everything that oppresses man but which is, above all,
liberation from sin and the Evil One.' (n 8–9.)

2. The Church, faithful to her mission, continues to present to the men of
every age, with the help of the Holy Spirit and under the Pope's guidance,
the message of salvation of her divine Founder.

This Dominican land was once the first to receive, and then to give
impetus to a grand enterprise of evangelization which deserves great
admiration and gratitude.

From the end of the fifteenth century, this beloved nation opens us to
the faith of Jesus Christ; to this it has remained faithful up to the present.
The Holy See, on its side, creates the first episcopal sees of America

16

precisely in this island, and subsequently the archiepiscopal and primatial see of Santo Domingo.

In a comparatively short period, the paths of faith crossed the Dominican land and the continent in all directions, laying the foundations of the heritage, become life, that we contemplate today in what was called the New World.

From the first moments of the discovery, there appears the concern of the Church to make the kingdom of God present in the heart of the new peoples, races, and cultures; in the first place, among your ancestors.

If we wish to express our well-deserved thanks to those who transplanted the seeds of faith, this tribute must be paid in the first place to the religious orders which distinguished themselves, even at the cost of offering their martyrs, in the task of evangelization: above all, the Dominicans, Franciscans, Augustinians, Mercedarians and then the Jesuits, who made the tender plant grow into a spreading tree. The fact is that the soil of America was prepared to receive the new Christian seeds by movements of spirituality of its own.

Nor is it a question, moreover, of a spreading of the faith detached from the life of those for whom it was intended; although it must always keep its essential reference to God. Therefore the Church in this island was the first to demand justice and to promote the defence of human rights in the lands that were opening to evangelization.

Lessons of humanism, spirituality and effort to raise man's dignity, are taught to us by Antonio Montesinos, Córdoba, Bartolomé de las Casas, echoed also in other parts by Juan de Zumárraga, Motolinia, Vasco de Quiroga, José de Anchieta, Toribio de Mogrovejo, Nóbrega and so many others. They are men in whom pulsates concern for the weak, for the defenceless, for the natives; subjects worthy of all respect as persons and as bearers of the image of God, destined for a transcendent vocation. The first International Law has its origin here with Francisco de Vitoria.

3. The fact is that the proclamation of the Gospel and human advancement cannot be dissociated — this is the great lesson valid also today. But for the Church, the former cannot be confused or exhausted, as some people claim, in the latter. That would be to close to man infinite spaces that God has opened to him. And it would be to distort the deep and complete meaning of evangelization, which is above all the proclamation of the Good News of Christ the Saviour.

The Church, an expert in humanity, faithful to the signs of the times, and in obedience to the pressing call of the last Council, wishes to continue today her mission of faith and defence of human rights. She calls upon Christians to commit themselves to the construction of a more just, human, and habitable world, which is not shut up within itself, but opens to God.

To construct this more just world means, among other things, making every effort in order that there will be no children without sufficient food, without education, without instruction; that there will be no young people without a suitable preparation; that, in order to live and to develop in a worthy way, there will be no peasants without land; that there will be no workers ill-treated or deprived of their rights; that there will be no systems that permit the exploitation of man by man or by the State; that there will be no corruption; that there will be no persons living in superabundance, while others through no fault of their own lack everything; that there will not be so many families badly formed, broken, disunited, receiving insufficient care; that there will be no injustice and inequality in the administration of justice; that there will be no one without the protection of the law, and that law will protect all alike; that force will not prevail over truth and law, but truth and law over force; and that economic or political matters will never prevail over human matters.

4. But do not be content with this more human world. Make a world that is explicitly more divine, more in accordance with God, ruled by faith, and in which this latter inspires the moral, religious, and social progress of man. Do not lose sight of the vertical dimension of evangelization. It has strength to liberate man, since it is the revelation of love. The love of the Father for men, for one and all; a love revealed in Jesus Christ. 'For God so loved the world that he gave his only son, that whoever believes in him should not perish but have eternal life.' (Jn. 3:16.)

Jesus Christ manifested this love above all in his hidden life — 'He has done all things well' (Mk. 7:37) — and by proclaiming the Gospel, then, by his death and resurrection, the paschal mystery in which man meets with his definitive vocation to eternal life, to union with God. This is the eschatological dimension of love.

Beloved Sons: I conclude by exhorting you always to be worthy of the faith that you have received. Love Christ, love man through him, and live devotion to our beloved Mother in heaven, whom you invoke with the beautiful name of Our Lady de la Altagracia (of the High Grace) and to whom the Pope wishes to leave a diadem as a homage of devotion. May she help you to walk towards Christ, preserving and fully developing the seed planted by your first evangelizers. This is what the Pope hopes from all of you. From you, sons of Cuba, present here, from you sons of Jamaica, Curaçao and the Antilles, Haiti, Venezuela, and the United States. Above all, from you, sons of the Dominican land. Amen

Later, in accordance with the announcement made in his sermon, the Pope presided over the ceremony of presentation of the diadem, offered by himself, to Our Lady of Altagracia at Higüey, the Protectress of the Dominican Republic. The miraculous statue of Our Lady of Altagracia, which was brought over specially from Higüey to the Cathedral for the occasion, is one of the most renowed relics in the history of the Dominicans dating back to the sixteenth century.

The second bishop of Santo Domingo was an Italian, Alessandro Geraldini, a humanist, poet and diplomat, who arrived there in 1520 and wrote some splendid Latin verses addressed to the Madonna: 'Hail full of grace, the Lord Eternal is with thee. And thou powerful Queen, Dove of our skies, shalt protect beneath thy wings, this land and this people.'

ADDRESS TO THE DIPLOMATIC CORPS

The Holy Father received members of the
Diplomatic Corps, accredited to the
Dominican Republic, at about 8 p.m.
when they made a courtesy visit to him
in the Nunciature.
He greeted them in a short speech:

Your Excellencies, Ladies and Gentlemen,

I would not like this short visit of mine to this country to pass without this meeting with you, who, for many varied reasons, are due a token of special attention on the part of the Pope.

You have wished to come to render you homage of respect and support as representatives of your respective countries, as wielders of authority at different levels in the Dominican nation, as persons bound to the Holy See by special ties, or as exponents of the cultural world.

I express my sincere gratitude to you all for your benevolent presence, as well as my deep appreciation of your respective functions. I wish you all success in your tasks, which can, and must, have a clear orientation of service for the common good, for the cause of human society, for the welfare of civil society and, for many, also of the Church. Many thanks.

Mexico *semper fidelis*

Friday 26 January

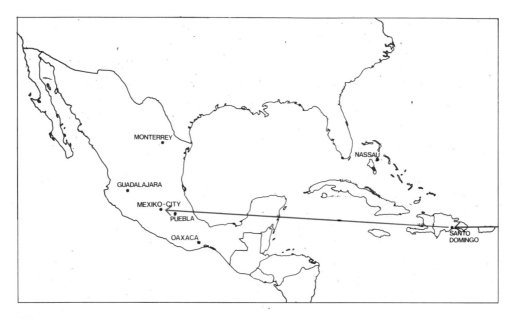

THE MORNING MASS

The Pope's second day in the Dominican Republic began early with a Mass which he said in the Cathedral at 6.45 a.m. This Mass was attended only by clergy and postulants and brought together, in the offering of the Eucharist, the Holy Father and those beloved sons 'in whom the Pope and the Church place their highest hopes'. After the Gospel, the Pope preached the following sermon:

Beloved Brothers and Sisters,

Blessed be the Lord who has brought me here, to this soil of the Dominican Republic, where fortunately, for the glory and praise of God in this new Continent, there also dawned the day of salvation. I have wished to come to this cathedral of Santo Domingo to be for a moment in your midst, beloved priests, deacons, men and women religious, and seminarians, to manifest to you my special affection for you all, in whom the Pope and the Church put their best hopes, in order that you may feel more joyful in faith, so that your pride in being what you are may overflow because of me (cf. Phil. 1:26).

Above all, however, I wish to join you in thanksgiving to God. Thanksgiving for the growth and zeal of this Church which has to its credit so many noble initiatives, and which shows such commitment in service of God and of men. I thank God with immense joy — to use the words of the Apostle Paul — 'for your partnership in the gospel from the first day until now. And I am sure that he who began a good work in you will bring it to completion at the day of Jesus Christ'. (ibid. 1:3ff.)

I really wish I had time to stay with you, to learn your names, and to hear from your lips 'that which overflows from the heart' (cf. Mt. 12:34), the marvellous things you have experienced in your soul — 'fecit mihi magna qui potens est' (Lk. 1:49): for he who is mighty has done great things for me — having been faithful to the meeting with the Lord. A meeting of preference on his side!

It is precisely this, the paschal meeting with the Lord, which I wish to propose to your reflection, in order to renew your faith and your enthusiasm in this eucharistic celebration; a personal, living meeting — with eyes wide open and a heart beating fast — with the Risen Christ (cf. Lk. 24:30), the objective of your love and of your whole life.

It sometimes happens that our harmony of faith with Jesus remains weak or fades — which is at once noticed by the faithful people, who are infected with sadness by it — because, although we bear him within us, it is sometimes in a way that is mingled with our human inclinations and reasonings (cf. ibid. 15), without letting all the magnificent light that he contains for us shine forth. On some occasions we may perhaps speak of him from the standpoint of some changing premises or data of a sociological, political, psychological, linguistical character; instead of drawing the basic criteria of our life and our activity from a Gospel lived with integrity, joy, with that immense confidence and hope that the Cross of Christ contains.

One thing is clear, beloved brothers: faith in the Risen Christ is not the result of technical knowledge or the fruit of scientific qualifications (cf. 1 Cor. 1:26). What is asked of us is to announce the death of Jesus and to proclaim his resurrection (cf. Liturgy). Jesus is alive. 'God raised him up, having loosed the bonds of death.' (Acts 2:24.) What was at the beginning a trembling murmur among the first witnesses, soon changed into the joyful experience of real life of those who 'ate and drank with him after he rose from the dead' (Acts 10:41f.). Yes, Christ really lives in the Church; he is in us, bearers of hope and immortality.

So if you have met Christ, live Christ, live with Christ! Proclaim him in the first person, as real witnesses: 'To me to live is Christ.' (Phil. 1:21.) Here, too, is real liberation: to proclaim Jesus free of bonds, present in men, who are transformed, made new creatures. Why is our testimony sometimes vain? Because we present Jesus without the whole attractive power of his Person; without revealing the riches of the sublime ideal that following him involves; because we do not always succeed in showing a conviction, expressed in real life, with regard to the stupendous value of our dedication to the great ecclesial cause that we serve.

Brothers and Sisters: Men must see in us the dispensers of God's mysteries (cf. 1 Cor. 4:1), the credible witnesses of his presence in the world. Let us think frequently that God, when he calls us, does not ask for just a part of our person, but he asks us for our whole person and all our vital energies in order to proclaim to men the joy and peace of the new life in Christ, in order to guide them to the meeting with him. Therefore, let our first care be to seek the Lord, and once we have met him, to ascertain where and how he lives, remaining with him the whole day (Jn. 1:39). Remaining with him, particularly, in the Eucharist, where Christ gives himself to us; and in prayer, by means of which we give ourselves to him. The Eucharist must be completed and prolonged through prayer, in our everyday affairs as a 'sacrifice of praise' (Roman Missal, Eucharistic Prayer I). In prayer, in familiar intercourse with God our Father, we discern better where is our strength and where is our weakness, because the Spirit comes to our help (cf. Rom. 8:26). The same Spirit speaks to us and gradually immerses us in the divine mysteries, in the plans of love for men which God carries out by means of our offer in his service.

Like St Paul, during a meeting at Troas to break bread, I, too, would continue to speak to you until midnight (cf. Acts 20:6ff.). I would have many more things to say but I cannot do so now. In the meantime I urge you to read carefully what I said recently in Rome, to the clergy, to men and women religious, and to seminarians. That will widen this meeting, which will continue spiritually with other similar ones in the next few days. May the Lord and our sweet Mother, the Blessed Virgin, accompany you always and fill your lives with great enthusiasm in the service of your noble ecclesial vocation.

Let us continue with Mass, placing on the table of offerings our desire to live the new life, our necessities and our supplications, the necessities and supplications of the Dominican Church and nation. Let us also put there the work and the fruits of the Third General Conference of the Latin American Episcopate at Puebla.

IN THE POOR QUARTER
OF LOS MINAS

The Pope's visit to the Los Minas slum,
on the outskirts of the capital, underlined
the apostolic concern of the Holy Father
for that part of humanity most in need of
help and solidarity. John Paul II
addressed the poor people of the quarter
from a platform in front of the parish
church of St Vincent de Paul, belonging
to the Lazarist Fathers.

Beloved Sons and Daughters of the 'Los Minas' district,

From the first moment of the preparation of my journey to your country, I
gave priority to a visit to this district of yours, in order to be able to meet
you.

And I wanted to come here just because it is a poor area, in order that
you might have the opportunity — I would say to which you have the best
claim — of being with the Pope. He sees in you a more living presence of
the Lord, who suffers in our neediest brothers, who continues to proclaim
blessed the poor in spirit, those who suffer for justice and are pure in
heart, who work for peace, have compassion, and keep their hope in Christ
the Saviour.

But on calling you to cultivate these spiritual and evangelical values, I
wish to make you think of your dignity as men and children of God. I
wish to encourage you to be rich in humanity, in love for the family, in
solidarity with others. At the same time I exhort you to develop more and
more the possibilities you have of obtaining a situation of greater human
and Christian dignity.

But what I have to say does not end here. The sight of the reality in
which you live must make so many people think of what can be done
effectively to remedy your condition.

On behalf of these brothers of ours, I ask all those who can do so to
help them to overcome their present situation, in order that, particularly
with a better education, they may improve their minds and their hearts,
and be architects of their own elevation and of a more advantageous
integration in society.

With this urgent appeal to consciences, the Pope encourages your
desires for advancement, and with great affection blesses you, your children
and relatives, and all the inhabitants of the district.

The Pope then talked to the
schoolchildren of the area and visited
two poor families some of whose
members were ill.

THE DEPARTURE FROM THE DOMINICAN REPUBLIC

At the end of his brief visit, at the Aeropuerto de las Americas just before leaving the Dominican Republic, the Pope addressed a message of farewell and thanksgiving to the President of the Republic:

Mr President,

With deep feeling on my part, the moment has come to have to leave this beloved land of the Dominican Republic, where the shortness of my stay has been compensated by a great abundance of intense religious and human experiences.

I have been able to admire some of the beauties of the country and its historico-religious monuments, and, above all, I have been able to see, to my deep satisfaction, the religious and human sentiment of its inhabitants.

These are unforgettable memories that accompany me and will continue to call up before me the beautiful days lived in this cradle of Catholicism in the New World.

Thank you, Mr President, for the innumerable attentions that have been bestowed on me and for your presence at this moment. Thanks to all the beloved Dominican people for their enthusiastic welcome, for their constant proofs of love for the Pope, and for their faithfulness to the Christian faith.

The Pope left the airport at 10.30 a.m. on board a DC10 of Mexican Airlines.

THE ARRIVAL IN MEXICO

The Pope arrived at Mexico City's International Airport at 12.50 p.m. local time. Thirteen minutes after touchdown, the Pope left the aircraft and, repeating his gesture in Santo Domingo, embraced the soil of Mexico to demonstrate his affection for its people who, in spite of hard times, have shown their attachment to their Christian faith with courage and constancy. The Cathedral bells and those of the entire country ring out a joyful peel. All the people are moved by an intense feeling of joy and enthusiasm. The Church is very much alive in the hearts of these people who welcome their spiritual leader, the Bishop of Rome. There followed a brief exchange of greetings with the ecclesiastical authorities and the President of the Republic. After this, the Pope was driven to the metropolitan Cathedral in an open car. The whole route was hung with flags; but it was far more densely lined by an immense throng of people. The Pope responded to the enthusiasm of the crowds with wide gestures of benediction. It took two hours to reach the Plaza de la Constitucion, the Zocalo. Inside the Cathedral, the Pope was welcomed by Cardinal José Salazar, President of the Episcopal Conference, and by the Archbishop of Mexico City, Ernesto Corripio. Then he began to celebrate the Mass.

After the Gospel, the Holy Father
delivered the following sermon:

Dear Brothers in the Episcopate and Beloved Sons,

It is only a few hours since with deep emotion I set foot for the first
time on this blessed land. And now I have the happiness of this meeting
with you, with the Mexican Church and people, on this *day of Mexico* as it
wishes to be.

It is a meeting which began with my arrival in this beautiful city; it
was extended as I passed through the streets and squares; it was intensified
on my entrance into this Cathedral. But it is here, in the celebration of the
Eucharistic Sacrifice, that it has its climax.

Let us put this meeting under the protection of the Mother of God, the
Virgin of Guadalupe, whom the Mexican people loves with the deepest
devotion.

To you bishops of this Church; to you priests, men and women
religious, seminarians, members of Secular Institutes, laity of Catholic and
apostolic movements; to you children, young people, adults, and the old;
to all of you, Mexicans, who have a splendid past of love for Christ, even
in the midst of trials; to you who bear in the depths of your heart devotion
to the Virgin of Guadalupe, the Pope wishes to speak today about
something which is, and must increasingly be an essential Christian and
Marian feature of yours: faithfulness to the Church.

Among the many titles bestowed on the Virgin throughout the
centuries by the filial love of Christians, there is one that has a very deep
meaning: Virgo Fidelis, the faithful Virgin. What does this faithfulness of
Mary's mean? What are the dimension of this faithfulness?

The first dimension is called *search*. Mary was faithful first of all when
she began, lovingly, to seek the deep sense of God's plan in her and for the
world. 'Quomodo fiet'? – How shall this be? – she asked the Angel of the
Annunciation. Already in the Old Testament the meaning of this search is
portrayed in an expression of outstanding beauty and extraordinary spiritual
content: 'To seek the face of the Lord.' There will not be faithfulness if it
is not rooted in this ardent, patient, and generous search; if there is not in

28

man's heart a question to which only God gives an answer, or rather, to which only God is the answer.

The second dimension of faithfulness is called reception, acceptance. The 'quomodo fiet?' is changed, on Mary's lips, to a 'fiat'. Let it be done, I am ready, I accept: this is the crucial moment of faithfulness, the moment in which man perceives that he will never completely understand the 'how'; that there are in God's plan more areas of mystery than of clarity; that, however he may try, he will never succeed in understanding it completely. It is then that man accepts the mystery, gives it a place in his heart, just as 'Mary kept all these things, pondering them in her heart' (Lk. 2:19; cf. Lk. 3:15). It is the moment when man abandons himself to the mystery, not with the resignation of one who capitulates before an enigma or an absurdity, but rather with the availability of one who opens up to be inhabited by something — by Someone! — greater than his own heart. This acceptance takes place, in short, through faith, which is the adherence of the whole being to the mystery that is revealed.

The third dimension of faithfulness is *consistency*. To live in accordance with what one believes. To adapt one's own life to the object of one's adherence. To accept misunderstandings, persecutions, rather than a break between what one practises and what one believes: this is consistency. Here is, perhaps, the deepest core of faithfulness.

But all faithfulness must pass the most exacting test: that of duration. Therefore the fourth dimension of faithfulness is *constancy*. It is easy to be consistent for a day or two. It is difficult and important to be consistent for one's whole life. It is easy to be consistent in the hour of enthusiasm, it is difficult to be so in the hour of tribulation. And only a consistency that lasts throughout the whole of life, can be called faithfulness. Mary's 'fiat' in the Annunciation finds its fullness in the silent 'fiat' that she repeats at the foot of the Cross. To be faithful means not betraying in the darkness what one has accepted in public.

Of all the teachings that the Virgin gives to her children in Mexico, the most beautiful and the most important one is perhaps this lesson of faithfulness. This faithfulness which the Pope delights in discovering and which he expects from the Mexican people.

It is said of my native country: 'Polonia semper fidelis'. I want to be able to say also: Mexico 'semper fidelis', always faithful!

In fact, the religious history of this nation is a history of faithfulness; faithfulness to the seeds of faith sown by the first missionaries; faithfulness to a simple but deep-rooted religious outlook, sincere to the point of sacrifice; faithfulness to Marian devotion; exemplary faithfulness to the Pope. I did not have to come to Mexico to know this faithfulness to the Vicar of Christ, because I knew it long ago; but I thank the Lord for being able to experience it in the fervour of your welcome.

At this solemn hour I would like to call upon you to strengthen this faithfulness, to make it stauncher. I would like to call you to express it in an intelligent and strong faithfulness to the Church today. And what will be the dimensions of this faithfulness if not the same as those of Mary's faithfulness?

The Pope who visits you, expects from you a generous and noble effort to know the Church better and better. The Second Vatican Council wished to be, above all, a Council on the Church. Take in your hands the documents of the Council, especially 'Lumen Gentium', study them with loving attention, with the spirit of prayer, to discover what the Spirit wished to say about the Church. In this way you will be able to realize that there is not – as some people claim – a 'new church', different or opposed to the 'old church', but that the Council wished to reveal more clearly the one Church of Jesus Christ, with new aspects, but still the same in its essence.

The Pope expects from you, moreover, loyal acceptance of the Church. To remain attached to incidental aspects of the Church, valid in the past but outdated today, would not be faithful in this sense. Nor would it be faithful to embark, in the name of an unenlightened prophetism, on the adventurous and utopian construction of a so-called Church of the future, disembodied from the present one. We must remain faithful to the Church which, born once and for all from God's plan, from the Cross, from the open sepulchre of the Risen Christ and from the grace of Pentecost, is born again every day, not from the people or from other rational categories, but from the same sources as those from which it was born originally. It is born today to construct with all the nations a people desirous of growing in faith, hope and brotherly love.

Likewise the Pope expects of you that your lives should be consistent with your membership of the Church. This consistency means being aware of one's identity as a Catholic and manifesting it, with complete respect, but also without wavering or fear. The Church today needs Christians ready to bear witness clearly to their condition, and who will play their part in the mission of the Church in the world, in all social environments, as a ferment of religiousness, justice, advancement of human dignity; trying to give the world an increase of spirit so that it may be a more human and brotherly world, looking towards God.

At the same time, the Pope hopes that your consistency will not be short-lived, but constant and persevering. To belong to the Church, to live in the Church, to be the Church, is something very demanding today. Sometimes it does not cost clear and direct persecution, but it may cost contempt, indifference, under-privilege. The danger of fear, weariness, and insecurity is, therefore, easy and frequent. Do not let yourselves be overcome by these temptations. Do not allow to vanish, as a result of any of these sentiments, the strength and the spiritual energy of your 'being the Church'. This is a grace which we must ask for, which we must be ready to receive with great inner poverty, and which we must begin to live every morning: and every day with greater fervour and intensity.

Dear Brothers and Sons: at this Eucharist which seals a meeting of the Servants of God with the soul and conscience of the Mexican people, the new Pope would like to gather from your lips, from your hands, and from your lives, a solemn commitment, in order to offer it to the Lord. The commitment of consecrated souls, of children, young people, adults, and the old; of cultured people and simple people, of men and women, of all: the commitment of faithfulness to Christ, to the Church of today. Let us put this intention and this commitment on the altar.

May the faithful Virgin, the Mother of Guadalupe, from whom we learn to know God's plan, his promise and his covenant, help us with her intercession to strengthen this commitment and to carry it out until the end of our lives, until the day when the voice of the Lord will say to us: 'Well done, good and faithful servant; enter into the joy of your master.' (Mt. 25:21–23.) Amen

At the end of his first Mass in Mexico,
from the balcony of the Cathedral, the
Holy Father addressed words of greeting
to the large crowd below:

Beloved Sons,

After receiving the welcoming greeting of Cardinal José Salazar and Archbishop Ernesto Corripio of this city, I have just finished the celebration of my first Mass on Mexican land, offered in this Metropolitan Cathedral.

I am very pleased to meet you here, and I greet one and all, priests, men and women religious, seminarians, adult persons, parents. But let my particularly cordial greeting go to the young, to the children, to the old and the sick.

Be assured that the Pope prayed at the Mass for all your intentions, asking the Lord to lead you by the path of moral rectitude and love of Christ and of the Church, to give you his consolation if you have any reason for sadness or sorrow, and to grant that you may live your Christian life authentically.

Above all, during these days when we will be close, you, too, pray for the Pope and for the Church. And we beseech the Virgin of Guadalupe fervently to help us on our way and to be our guide to her Son and our Brother, Jesus.

With great affection, the Pope gives his blessing to you all.

THE MESSAGE TO THE
DIPLOMATIC CORPS

Soon after 3 p.m., John Paul II went to
the Apostolic Delegation where the
Diplomatic Corps accredited to the
Mexican Government were waiting to be
presented to him. To them he made a
short speech in which he underlined the
need for peace and for furthering human
rights.

Your Excellencies, illustrious members of the Diplomatic Corps,

I am really happy that in the midst of the programme, so full, of my visit
to Mexico, there is this meeting of greeting to such a distinguished group
of persons as is the Diplomatic Corps accredited in Mexico City.

On many occasions the Holy See has shown its high esteem and
appreciation for the function of diplomatic representatives. I, too, did so at
the beginning of my pontificate. And I gladly repeat before you today my
positive evaluation of this noble task, when it is put in the service of the
great cause of peace, understanding among nations, and a reciprocally
advantageous exchange in so many fields of interdependence in the
international community.

You and I, Gentlemen, have also a common concern: the good of
humanity and the future of peoples and of all men. If your mission is in
the first place the defence and advancement of the legitimate interests of
your respective nations, the inescapable interdependency which binds the
peoples of the world together more and more every day, I call upon all
diplomats to become, with an ever new and original spirit, architects of the
understanding among peoples, of international security, and of peace
among nations.

You are well aware that all human societies, national and international,
will be judged in this field of peace by the contribution they have made to
man's development and to respect of his fundamental rights. If society
must guarantee in the first place the exercise of a real right to existence, it
is not possible to separate from this right another equally fundamental
exigency, which we might call the right to peace and security.

Every human being, in fact, aspires to conditions of peace which will
permit a harmonious development of future generations, protected from the
terrible calamity that war will always be, protected from recourse to force
or to any other form of violence.

To guarantee peace for all the inhabitants of our planet means seeking
– with all the generosity and dedication, with all the dynamism and
perseverance, of which men of good will are capable – all the concrete
means calculated to promote peaceful and brotherly relations, not only on
the international plane, but also on the plane of the different continents
and regions; in which it will sometimes be easier to obtain results which,
though limited, are none the less important. Peace achievements on the

regional plane will constitute, in fact, an example and an invitation for the whole international community.

I would like to exhort each of you and, through you, all the leaders of the nations which you represent, to eliminate fear and mistrust and replace them with mutual trust, welcome vigilance, and brotherly collaboration. This new atmosphere in relations among the nations will make it possible to discover areas of agreement that are often unsuspected.

Allow the Pope, this humble pilgrim of peace that I am, to call your attention again to the appeal I made, in my message for the Day of Peace, to all those responsible for the fate of nations: do not hesitate to commit yourselves personally for peace with acts of peace, each in your own sphere and in your own sphere of responsibility. Create new and bold acts that are manifestations of respect, brotherhood, confidence and welcome. By means of these acts you will use all your personal and professional capacities in the service of the great cause of peace. And I promise you that, along the way to peace, you will always find God accompanying you.

In the context of this appeal, I would like to communicate to you a particular wish. I am referring to the growing number of refugees all over the world and to the tragic situation of the refugees in South East Asia. Exposed not only to the risks of a dangerous journey, the latter also meet with the refusal of their request for asylum, or have to wait for a long time before they get the possibility of beginning a new life in a country ready to welcome them. The solution of this tragic problem is the responsibility of all nations, and I desire that the competent international organizations may be able to rely on the comprehension and help of countries in all continents — especially a continent such as Latin America, which has always honoured its centuries-long tradition of hospitality — in order to deal openly with this humanitarian problem.

Allow me therefore to encourage you in this task, aware as you are of the deep sense of professional ethics that must accompany this service of sacrifice, sometimes not understood, to society.

In order that God may bless your efforts, your persons and families, I invoke the protection of the Almighty.

A private meeting with President Lopez Portillo at his residence, Los Pinos, brought to a close the Pope's first day in Mexico. The Pope remained in the presidential palace from 6.45 to 8 p.m. Only the closest collaborators of the Pope and the President were present during their conversation and no communiqué was released; but it is reasonable to suppose that both sides examined problems of peace, international co-operation and the promotion of social justice in the world.

Help us to Teach Truth

Saturday 27 January

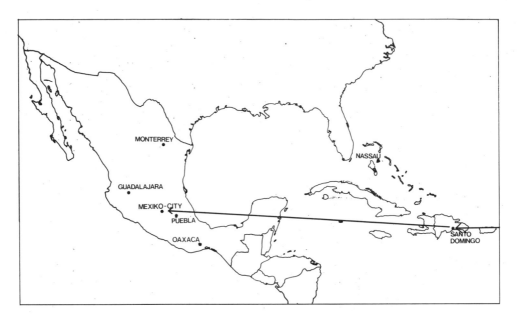

MORNING SONGS

The second day of John Paul II's stay in Mexico, Saturday 27th, had a musical start, with folklore groups and choirs appearing early, in front of the Apostolic Delegate's residence where the Pope was staying, to sing their famous *mañanitas* or morning songs.

Even earlier, during the small hours of the night, a crowd had begun to gather round the residence so that it was only with difficulty that members of the Polish community in Mexico, who has an audience with the Holy Father at 9 a.m. were able to gain access to the Apostolic Delegate's house. The crowd surrounded the house with their enthusiastic cries of 'Long live the Pope, Long live Mexico'.

A MEETING WITH THE POLISH COMMUNITY

A Polish interlude on Mexican territory followed. The Polish community numbers about four hundred people who emigrated soon after the beginning of the Second World War. In addition, other Poles from the United States and Guatemala came to Mexico City for the occasion. The meeting with the Pope took place at about 8.30 a.m. in the garden of the Apostolic Delegation. Among those present were many children dressed in Polish costume. The Pope addressed a message of greeting to his countrymen from a dais erected in the middle of the garden over which flew a large Polish flag and, before conferring his blessing on the visitors, he spoke personally with each oné of them and received many gifts from them.

AT THE SHRINE OF GUADALUPE

An ocean of human beings, estimated at five million, waited under a burning sun to see the Pope go by along the 20 kilometre route from the Apostolic Delegation to the Shrine of Our Lady of Guadalupe, north of the immense city. It took the Pope's long, white, open station-wagon almost three hours, going at walking pace between the two lines of excited crowds, to cover the distance. At 11.30 a.m. the church bells of Guadalupe were ringing continuously to greet the arrival of the Pope in the square in front of the sanctuary. Not less than 200,000 people were assembled here to give the Holy Father a tumultuous welcome. Many of the faithful made sure of seeing the Pope by occupying their places 24 hours earlier, and they greeted him with thousands of flags, papal and Mexican but also Italian and Polish.

On reaching the centre of the square, John Paul II halted for a few minutes to acknowledge the welcome of the crowd, and then made a short visit to the old baroque shrine. At 12.20 p.m. he entered the new basilica to concelebrate the

Mass with three hundred or more Latin American bishops, who were taking part in the Conference of Puebla de Los Angeles. The new basilica, in which the miraculous effigy of Our Lady of Guadalupe has been placed, is a modern construction of steel and reinforced concrete which somewhat resembles a volcano or, more likely a *sombrero*. The papal throne was placed beneath the painting of the Madonna of Guadalupe, called affectionately by the Mexicans *la Morenita* because of its dark colour. As the Pope entered the church, the choir and congregation sang traditional Mexican hymns to Our Lady. There followed the solemn concelebration of the Mass which officially inaugurated the third General Conference of the Latin American Bishops. In his sermon the Pope said:

Hail Mary!

1. Dear brothers in the episcopate and dear sons and daughters, how deep is my joy that the first steps of my pilgrimage, as Successor of Paul VI and John Paul I, bring me precisely here. They bring me to you, Mary, in this shrine of the people of Mexico and of the whole of Latin America, the shrine in which for so many centuries your motherhood has been manifested.

Hail Mary!

It is with immense love and reverence that I utter these words, words so simple and at the same time so marvellous. No one will ever be able to greet you in a more wonderful way than the way in which the Archangel once greeted you at the moment of the Annunciation. Hail Mary, full of grace, the Lord is with thee. I repeat these words, words that so many hearts ponder upon and so many lips utter throughout the world. We here present utter them together, and we are aware that these are the words with which God himself, through his messenger, greeted you, the woman promised in the Garden of Eden, chosen from eternity as the Mother of the Word, the Mother of Divine Wisdom, the Mother of the Son of God.

Hail, Mother of God!

2. Your Son Jesus Christ is our Redeemer and Lord. He is our Teacher. All of us gathered here are his disciples. We are the Successors of the Apostles, of those to whom the Lord said: 'Go therefore and make disciples of all nations, baptizing them in the name of the Father and of the Son and of the Holy Spirit, teaching them to observe all that I have commanded you; and lo, I am with you always, to the close of the age.' (Mt. 28:19–20.)

Gathered here together, the Successor of Peter and the successors of the Apostles, we ponder on how admirably these words have been fulfilled in this land.

In fact, scarcely twenty years after the work of evangelization was begun in the New World in 1492, the Faith reached Mexico. Soon afterwards, the first archiepiscopal see was established, presided over by Juan de Zumárraga, supported by other great evangelizers, who were to extend Christianity over very wide areas.

No less glorious religious epics were to be written in the Southern Hemisphere by men such as Saint Turibius of Mogroviejo and a long list of others who would deserve to be mentioned here at length. The paths of the Faith steadily stretched further, until at the end of the first century of evangelization the episcopal sees numbered more than seventy, with some four million Christians. This singular undertaking was to continue for a long time, until today, after five centuries of evangelization, it embraces almost a half of the entire Catholic Church, which has struck root in the culture of the people of Latin America and forms part of their own identity.

And with the achievement in these lands of Christ's mandate, with the multiplication everywhere of the children of divine adoption through the grace of baptism, the Mother appeared too. In fact, the Son of God, and your Son, from the Cross indicated a man to you, Mary, and said: 'Behold, your son' (Jn. 19:26). And in that man he entrusted to you every person, he entrusted everyone to you. And you, who at the moment of the Annunciation, concentrated the whole programme of your life in those simple words: 'Behold I am the handmaid of the Lord; let it be to me according to your word' (Lk. 1:38). embrace everyone, draw close to everyone, seek everyone out with motherly care.

Thus is accomplished what the last Council said about your presence in the mystery of Christ and the Church. In a wonderful way you are always found in the mystery of Christ, your only Son, because you are present wherever men and women, his brothers and sisters, are present, wherever the Church is present.

In fact, when the first missionaries who reached America from lands of eminent Marian tradition taught the rudiments of Christian faith, they also taught love for you, the Mother of Jesus and of all people. And ever since the time that the Indian Juan Diego spoke of the sweet Lady of Tepeyac, you, Mother of Guadalupe, have entered decisively into the Christian life of the people of Mexico. No less has been your presence in other places, where your children invoke you with tender names, as Our Lady of Altagracia, of the Aparecida, of Luján, and with many other no less affectionate names, not to give an unending list — names by which in each nation and even in each region the peoples of Latin America express their most profound devotion to you, and under which you protect them in their pilgrimage of faith.

The Pope — who comes from a country in which your images, especially one, that of Jasna Gora, are also a sign of your presence in the nation's life and its hazardous history — is particularly sensitive to this sign of your presence here, in the Life of the People of God in Mexico, in its history, a history which has also been not easy, and at times even dramatic. But you are also equally present in the life of the many other peoples of Latin America, presiding over and guiding not only their past, whether remote or recent, but also the present moment, with its uncertainties and shadows. The Pope perceives in the depths of his heart the special bonds that link you with this people and this people with you. This people, that gives you the affectionate name of *La Morenita.* This people, and indirectly the whole of this vast continent, lives its spiritual unity thanks to the fact that you are its Mother. A Mother who, through her love, creates, preserves and increases closeness between her children.

Hail, Mother of Mexico!
Mother of Latin America!

3. We meet here at this exceptional and wonderful hour in the history of the world. We have come to this place, conscious that we are at a crucial moment. With this meeting of Bishops we wish to link ourselves with the previous Conference of the Latin American Bishops that took place ten years ago at Medellín together with the Eucharistic Congress at Bogotá, which Pope Paul VI of indelible memory took part in. We have come here not so much to examine again, ten years later, the same problem, but rather to review it in a new way, at a new place, and at a new moment of history.

We wish to take as our point of departure what is contained of that Conference. And at the same time we wish, on the basis of the experiences of the last ten years and of the development of thought and in the light of the experiences of the whole Church, to take a correct and necessary step forward.

The Medellín Conference took place shortly after the close of Vatican II, the Council of our century, and the objective was to take up again the Council's essential plans and content, in order to apply them and make them a directing force in the concrete situation of the Church in Latin America.

Without the Council the Medellín meeting would not have been possible; that meeting was meant to be an impulse of spiritual renewal, a new 'spirit' in the face of the future in full ecclesial fidelity in interpreting the signs of the times in Latin America. The evangelizing intention was quite clear. It is obvious in the sixteen themes dealt with, grouped about three great mutually complementary topics, namely human advancement, evangelization and growth in faith, and the visible Church and her structures.

By opting for the man of Latin America seen in his entirety, by showing preferential yet not exclusive love for the poor, and by encouraging integral liberation of individuals and peoples, Medellín, the Church present in that place, was a call of hope towards more Christian and more human goals.

But more than ten years have passed. And interpretations have been given that have been at times contradictory, not always correct, not always beneficial for the Church. The Church is therefore looking for the ways that will enable her to understand more deeply and fulfil more zealously the mission she has been given by Christ Jesus.

Much importance in this regard is found in the sessions of the Synod of Bishops held in the years since then, especially the session of 1974, which concentrated on Evangelization; its conclusions were put together later, in a lively and encouraging manner, in Paul VI's Apostolic Exhortation *Evangelii Nuntiandi*.

This is the theme that we are today placing before us for study by proposing to consider 'Evangelization in Latin America's Present and Future.'

As we meet in this sacred place to begin our work, we see before our eyes the upper room in Jerusalem, where the Eucharist was instituted.

44

After the Lord's Ascension the Apostles returned to the same upper room in order to devote themselves to prayer, together with Mary, the Mother of Christ, and so prepare their hearts to receive the Holy Spirit at the moment of the Church's birth.

That is also why we have come here. We also are awaiting the descent of the Holy Spirit, who will make us see the paths of evangelization by which the Church must continue and must be reborn in this great continent of ours. We also wish today and in the days ahead to devote ourselves to prayer with Mary, the Mother of our Lord and Master — with you, Mother of hope, Mother of Guadalupe.

4. Let me, John Paul II, Bishop of Rome and Pope, together with my Brothers in the Episcopate representing the Church in Mexico and the whole of Latin America, at this solemn moment entrust and offer to you, the handmaid of the Lord, the whole heritage of the Gospel, the Cross, and the Resurrection, of which we are all witnesses, apostles, teachers, and bishops.

O Mother, help us to be faithful stewards of the great mysteries of God. Help us to teach the truth proclaimed by your Son and to spread love, which is the chief commandment and the first fruit of the Holy Spirit. Help us to strengthen our brethren in faith, help us to awaken hope in eternal life. Help us to guard the great treasures stored in the souls of the People of God entrusted to us.

We offer you the whole of this People of God. We offer you the Church in Mexico and in the whole continent. We offer it to you as your own. You have entered so deeply into the hearts of the faithful through that sign of your presence constituted by your image in the Shrine of Guadalupe; be at home in these hearts, for the future also. Be at home in our families, our parishes, missions, dioceses, and in all the peoples.

Do this through the Holy Church, for she, in imitation of you, Mother, wishes in her turn to be a good mother and to care for souls in all their needs, by proclaiming the Gospel, administering the Sacraments, safeguarding family life with the sacrament of Matrimony, gathering all into the Eucharistic community by means of the Holy Sacrament of the altar, and by being lovingly with them from the cradle until they enter eternity.

O Mother, awaken in the younger generation readiness for the exclusive service of God. Implore for us abundant local vocations to the priesthood and the consecrated life.

O Mother, strengthen the faith of our brothers and sisters in the laity, so that in every field of social, professional, cultural and political life they may act in accordance with the truth and the law brought by your Son to mankind, in order to lead everyone to eternal salvation and, at the same time, to make life on earth more human, more worthy of man.

The Church that is carrying out her task among the American nations, the Church in Mexico, wishes to serve this sublime cause with all her strength and with renewed missionary spirit. Mother, enable us to serve the Church in truth and justice. Make us follow this way ourselves and lead others, without ever straying along twisted paths and dragging others with us.

We offer and entrust to you everybody and everything for which we have pastoral responsibility, confident that you will be with us and will help us to carry out what your Son has told us to do (cf. Jn. 2:5). We bring you this unlimited trust; with this trust I, John Paul II, with all my Brothers in the Episcopate of Mexico and Latin America, wish to bind you still more strongly to our ministry, to the Church and to the life of our nations. We wish to place in your hands the whole of our future, the future of evangelization in Latin America.

Queen of the Apostles, accept our readiness to serve unreservedly the cause of your Son, the cause of the Gospel and the cause of peace based on justice and love between individuals and peoples.

Queen of Peace, save the nations and peoples of the whole continent — they have so much trust in you — from wars, hatred and subversion.

Make everybody, whether they are rulers or subjects, learn to live in peace, educate themselves for peace, and do what is demanded by justice and respect for the rights of every person, so that peace may be firmly established.

Accept our trustful offering, O handmaid of the Lord. May your maternal presence in the mystery of Christ and of the Church become a source of joy and freedom for each and every one, source of that freedom through which 'Christ has set us free' (Gal. 5:1), and in the end a source of that peace that the world cannot give but which is only given by him, by Christ (cf. Jn. 14:27).

Finally, O Mother, recalling and confirming the gesture of my Predecessors Benedict XIV and Pius X, who proclaimed you Patroness of Mexico and of the whole of Latin America, I present to you a diadem in the name of all your Mexican and Latin American children, that you may keep them under your protection, preserve their harmony in faith and their fidelity to Christ, your Son. Amen

SPEECH TO PRIESTS
AND RELIGIOUS

To the priests and religious of Mexico,
who attended the meeting with the Pope
at 5 p.m. in the Basilica of Our Lady at
Guadalupe in large numbers, the Holy
Father addressed the following speech:

Beloved priests, diocesan and religious,

One of the meetings I was most looking forward to during my visit to
Mexico is that I have with you, here in the Sanctuary of our venerated and
beloved Mother of Guadalupe.

See in it a proof of the Pope's affection and solicitude. He, as the
Bishop of the whole Church, is aware of your irreplaceable role. He feels
very close to those who are keystones in the ecclesial task, as the main
collaborators of the Bishops, participants in Christ's saving powers,
witnesses, proclaimers of his Gospel, encouraging the faith and apostolic
vocation of the People of God. And here I do not wish to forget so many
other consecrated souls, precious collaborators, though without the priestly
character, in many important sectors of the Church apostolate.

Not only do you have a special presence in the Church apostolate, but
also your love for man through God is conspicuous among students at
different levels, among the sick and those in need of assistance, among men
of culture, among the poor who demand understanding and support,
among so many persons who have recourse to you in search of advice and
encouragement.

For your self-sacrificing dedication to the Lord and to the Church, for
your closeness to man, receive my thanks in Christ's name.

Servants of a sublime cause, the fate of the Church largely depends on
you in the sectors entrusted to your pastoral care. That makes it necessary
for you to be deeply aware of the greatness of the mission you have received
and of the necessity of better and better adapting yourselves to it.

It is a question, in fact, beloved brothers and sons, of the Church of
Christ — what respect and love this must inspire in us! — which you have to
serve joyfully in holiness of life (cf. Eph. 4:13).

This high and exacting service cannot be carried out without a clear
and deep-rooted conviction of your identity as priests of Christ, depositaries
and administrators of God's mysteries, instruments of salvation for men,
witnesses of a kingdom which begins in this world but is completed in the
next. In the light of these certainties of faith, why doubt about your own
identity? Why hesitate about the value of your own life? Why waver on
the path which you have chosen?

To preserve or strengthen this firm and persevering conviction, look at
the model, Christ; renew the supernatural values in your existence, ask for
strength from above, in the assiduous and trusting conversation of prayer.
It is indispensable for you, today as yesterday. And also be faithful to
frequent practice of the Sacrament of Reconciliation, to daily meditation,

to devotion to the Virgin by means of the recitation of the Rosary. In a word, cultivate union with God by means of a deep inner life. Let this be your first commitment. Do not be afraid that the time dedicated to the Lord will take anything away from your apostolate. On the contrary, it will be the source of fruitfulness in the ministry.

You are persons who have made the Gospel a profession of life. You must draw from the Gospel the essential principles of faith — not mere psychological or sociological principles — which will produce a harmonious synthesis between spirituality and ministry; without permitting a 'professionalization' of the latter, without diminishing the esteem that your celibacy or consecrated chastity, accepted for love of the Kingdom in an unlimited spiritual fatherhood (1 Cor. 4:15), must win for you. 'To them (priests) we owe our blessed regeneration' — St John Chrysostom affirms — 'and knowledge of true freedom' (On the Priesthood, 4–6).

You are participants in Christ's ministerial priesthood for the service of the unity of the community. A service which is realized by virtue of the authority received to direct the People of God, to forgive sins and to offer the Eucharistic Sacrifice (cf. *Lumen Gentium,* 10; *Presbyterorum Ordinis,* 2)! A specific priestly service, which cannot be replaced in the Christian community by the common priesthood of the faithful, which is essentially different from the former (*Lumen Gentium,* 10)!

You are members of a particular Church, whose centre of unity is the Bishop (*Christus Dominus,* 28), towards whom every priest must observe an attitude of communion and obedience. Religious, on their side, with regard to pastoral activities, cannot deny to the local hierarchy their loyal collaboration and obedience, on the pretext of exclusive dependence on the universal Church (cf. *Christus Dominus,* 34; *Joint Document of the Sacred Congregation for Religious and for Secular Institutes and of the Sacred Congregation for the Bishops,* 14 May 1978). Far less would it be admissible for priests or religious to practice a parallel to that of the Bishops — the only authentic teachers in the faith — or of the Episcopal Conferences.

You are servants of the People of God, servants of faith, administrators and witnesses of Christ's love for men; a love that is not partisan, that excludes no one, although it is addressed preferably to the poorest. In this connection, I wish to remind you of what I said not long ago to the Superiors General of the Religious in Rome: 'The soul that lives in habitual contact with God and moves within the ardent ray of his love, is able to defend itself easily against the temptation of particularisms and contrasts that create the risk of painful divisions; it is able to interpret in the correct light of the Gospel the options for the poorest and for each of the victims of human selfishness, without giving way to socio-political radicalisms which are seen in the long run to be inopportune and self-defeating'. (24 November 1978.)

You are spiritual guides who endeavour to direct and improve the hearts of the faithful in order that, converted, they may live love for God and their neighbour and commit themselves to the betterment of man and to increasing his dignity.

You are priests and religious; you are not social or political leaders or

officials of a temporal power. For this reason I repeat to you: 'Let us not be under the illusion that we are serving the Gospel if we "dilute" our charism through an exaggerated interest in the wide field of temporal problems.' (Address to the Clergy of Rome.) Let us not forget that temporal leadership can easily be a source of division, while the priest must be a sign and agent of unity and brotherhood. Secular functions are the specific field of action of laymen, who have to improve temporal matters with the Christian spirit (*Apostolicam Actuositatem,* 4).

Beloved priests and religious: I would say many other things to you, but I do not wish to make this meeting too long. I will say some things on another occasion, and I refer you to them.

I conclude repeating to you my great confidence in you. I have great hopes in your love for Christ and for men. There is a great deal to be done. Let us set out with renewed enthusiasm; united with Christ, under the motherly gaze of the Virgin, Our Lady of Guadalupe, the sweet mother of priests and religious. With the affectionate blessing of the Pope, for you and for all the priests and religious of Mexico.

Many Mexican nuns were present at a
meeting with the Pope which took place
at 6.30 p.m. in the 'Miguel Angel'
College, where the Holy Father addressed
them as follows:

Beloved Religious Daughters of Mexico,

This meeting of the Pope with Mexican Sisters, which was to have been
celebrated in the Basilica of Our Mother of Guadalupe, takes place here in
her spiritual presence; before her, the perfect model of woman, the best
example of a life dedicated entirely to her Son the Saviour, in a constant
inner attitude of faith, hope, and loving dedication to a supernatural
mission.

In this privileged place and before this figure of the Virgin, the Pope
wishes to pass some moments with you, the many Sisters present here, who
represent the more than twenty thousand scattered all over Mexico and
outside their homeland.

You are a very important force within the Church and within society
itself, spread in innumerable sectors such as the schools and colleges, the
clinics and hospitals, the field of charity and welfare, parish works,
catechesis, the groups of apostolate, and so many others. You belong to
different religious families, but with the same ideal within different
charisms: to follow Christ, to be a living witnesses to his everlasting
message.

Yours is a vocation which deserves the highest esteem on the part of
the Pope and the Church, yesterday as today. For this reason I wish to
express to you my joyful confidence in you, and encourage you not to be
discouraged along the way that you have undertaken, which is worth
continuing with renewed spirit and enthusiasm. Be assured that the Pope
accompanies you with his prayer, and that he delights in your faithfulness
to your vocation, to Christ and to the Church.

At the same time, however, allow me to add some reflections which I
propose for your consideration and examination.

It is certain that a praiseworthy spirit of faithfulness to their own
ecclesial commitment prevails in a good many Sisters, and that aspects of
great vitality can be seen in religious life with a return to a more
evangelical view, growing solidarity among religious families, greater
closeness to the poor, who are given rightful priority of attention. These
are reasons for joy and optimism.

But there are not lacking, either, examples of confusion with regard to
the very essence of consecrated life and one's own charism. Sometimes
prayer is abandoned and it is replaced by action; the vows are interpreted
according to the secularizing mentality which dulls the religious
motivations of one's own state; community life is abandoned with a certain

irresponsibility; socio-political attitudes are adopted as the real aim to pursue, even with well-defined ideological radicalizations.

And when the certainties of faith are sometimes dimmed, motives are put forward such as the seeking of new horizons and experiences, perhaps with the pretext of being closer to men, maybe concrete groups, chosen with criteria that are not always evangelical.

Beloved Sisters: never forget that to maintain a clear concept of the value of your consecrated life you need a deep vision of faith, which is nourished and preserved with prayer (cf. *Perfectae Caritatis,* 6). This faith will enable you to overcome all uncertainty with regard to your own identity, and will keep you faithful to that vertical dimension which is essential for you in order to identify you with Christ from the beatitudes, and in order to be true witnesses to the Kingdom of God for men of the modern world.

Only with this concern for the interests of Christ (cf. 1 Cor. 7:32) will you be capable of giving to the charism of prophecy its suitable dimension of witness to the Lord: without options for the poor and needy which do not spring from the criteria of the Gospel, but are inspired by socio-political motivations which — as I said recently to the Mothers Superiors General in Rome — turn out in the long run to be inopportune and self-defeating.

You have chosen as way of life the pursuit of some values which are not merely human ones, although you must also esteem the latter in their rightful measure. You have opted for service of others for love of God. Never forget that the human being is not exhausted in the earthly dimension only. You as professionals of faith and experts in the sublime knowledge of Christ (cf. Phil. 3:8), open them to the call and dimension of eternity in which you yourselves must live.

I would have many other things to tell you. Take as said to you what I indicated to the Mothers Superiors General in my address of 16 November last. How much you can do today for the Church and for mankind! They are waiting for your generous commitment, the dedication of your free heart, expanding in an unsuspected way its potentialities of love in a world that is losing the capacity of altruism, self-sacrificing and disinterested love. Remember, in fact, that you are mystical brides of Christ and of Christ crucified (cf. 2 Cor. 4:5).

The Church repeats to you today her trust: be living witnesses to this new civilization of love, which my predecessor Paul VI rightly proclaimed.

In order that strength from above may support you in this magnificent and hopeful enterprise, that it will keep you, in renewed spiritual youth faithful to these resolutions, I accompany you with a special Blessing, which I extend to all the Sisters in Mexico.

With the Concern of a Pastor and a Father's Love

Sunday 28 January

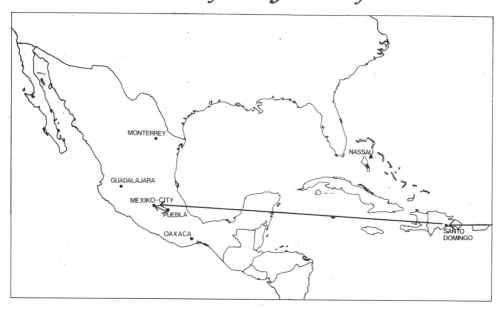

THE JOURNEY TO PUEBLA

John Paul II set off for Puebla early in the morning. Mexico City, the largest in the world, seemed to have been up all night. Everybody wanted to see the Pope, to greet him, to thank him. The Bishop Primate of Rome has, in a flash, conquered the hearts of the Mexicans, who admire in him a pontiff of unshakeable faith, a supreme witness to truth, an indefatigable apostle of the Gospel.

The distance between the capital and Puebla is 135 kilometres along a modern motorway. The journey can be completed easily in just over an hour. But the Pope was not in a hurry, like a business man. He came to Mexico as a pastor and as Head of the Catholic Church. He wanted to meet his sons, greet them, talk to them, including the outcasts of modern civilization. As things turned out, he had to advance through a veritable sea of humanity, so numerous were the prople who lined the route to see the Pope. 'I can't believe my eyes' exclaimed an excited commentator of the local television network. His astonishment was due to the fact that perhaps for the first and only time the Mexicans had broken with an age-old custom. 'How is it possible', asked the commentator, 'for all these Mexicans to be up and about when it is only 7 o'clock?' But it was not an outburst of mere curiosity or of passing enthusiasm. In John Paul II Mexicans recognized a standard-bearer of the Faith, and through him they renewed their faith and their loyalty to the Church, to Christ and to His Gospel.

By now the crowd had named John Paul II 'the Mexican Pope', such was the place he occupied in their hearts. They would not leave him alone. Many tried to accompany the papal procession but most remained with him in prayer and thanksgiving.

Though the departure was delayed by half an hour, this did not reduce the demands of the programme. The citizens of Mexico, and others who came to see him, retain the image of him which was observed during the Mass in the Sanctuary of Our Lady of Guadalupe — a man absorbed in prayer, moved to tears, his head between his hands.

The procession halted a while at the bridge of San Salvador El Verde. The nearby village, whose name derives from both Aztec and Christian roots, San Martin Texmelcan, is inhabited by Indians. They showed their pleasure by decorating their houses with yellow bunting. The Indians too are sons of the Church, the spiritual sons of the Pope. John Paul II got out of his car to have a chat with them, for the Church loves them, keeps them in her care, preaches the Gospel to them.

In the course of this journey many poor peasants were encountered, those for whom the Church has a special responsibility. For their betterment, which is also for the advancement of mankind, the Church has fought with all the authority which it commands through a vast network of cultural, social and pastoral institutions, which provide one of the most important chapters of its history in Latin America. Like the *Indios,* the *Campesinos* have few gifts to offer, but these are the most authentically evangelical gifts of all. They are the gifts of those who have nothing else to offer, the most acceptable and the most precious of gifts for the Kingdom of Heaven.

And so the Pope's car finally reaches the outskirts of Puebla. At San Miguel Xoytla the programme prescribed a halt so that the Pope might receive a formal welcome from a working man. The Pope was visibly moved. He himself has had direct experience of the industrial workers' world. He knows what strength a nation can derive from its working class and what a contribution it can make to economic progress. He is aware, nevertheless, of the tensions, the alienation, the exploitation to which it is exposed. His constant appeals for respect for human rights, for an opening to Christ of political and economic systems, are specifically directed towards obtaining for the working man the recognition of his dignity as a collaborator with God.

AT PUEBLA

The people of Puebla had been waiting in the streets and squares all through the night. The most crowded places were the areas round the Cathedral and the Palafoxian Seminary. At midday the ten bells of the northern tower of the city announced the arrival of the papal cortège. Immediately, the bells of the three hundred churches of the city joined in with their chimes. After passing through the main streets of the town in the open car, the Pope halted briefly at the Cathedral, though without mounting to the balcony to bless the crowd because he was behindhand with his programme. As he went on again, his car passed under banners in Spanish and Polish bearing the words 'Young people, Christ is your King', and 'Welcome'. From the balconies along the route came a downpour of confetti. Every inch of space on the walls was covered with flags or posters bearing the picture of the Pope, the work of university students or of members of the various Catholic associations. People had clambered up on high gates, on street-lamps, on traffic lights.

At 1 p.m. the Pope arrived at the Palafoxian Seminary where he was given an ovation by over 300,000 people in the square. A small girl presented him with a bunch of flowers. After vesting himself, the Pope moved in procession to an open-air altar while the crowd chanted 'Puebla loves the Pope' and *'Karol Wojtyla, tu es Petrus'*. It was now 1.25 p.m., one and a half hours behind the timetable laid down in the programme. The Mexican and Polish flags were flying from the top of the building. The Pope said Mass in an atmosphere of reverent devotion, only interrupted during his sermon on the Family, by the applause which greeted the principal passages.

Beloved Sons and Daughters,

Puebla de los Angeles: today the sonorous and expressive name of your city is on millions of lips throughout Latin America and all over the world. Your city becomes a symbol and sign for the Latin American Church. It is here, in fact, that from today the Bishops of the whole Continent, convened by the Successor of Peter, gather to reflect on the mission of Pastors in this part of the world, in this extraordinary hour of history.

The Pope has desired to come up to this high place from where the whole of Latin America seems to open up. And it is with the impression of contemplating the picture of each one of the nations that the Pope has wished to celebrate the Eucharistic Sacrifice on this altar erected on the mountains, to invoke on this Conference, on its participants and on its work, the light, the warmth and all the gifts of the Spirit of God, the Spirit of Jesus Christ.

There is nothing more natural and necessary than to invoke him on this occasion. The great Assembly which is opening is, in fact, an ecclesial meeting in its deepest essence: ecclesial because of those who meet here, the Pastors of the Church of God in Latin America; ecclesial because of the subject it studies, the mission of the Church in the continent; ecclesial because of its aims: to make more living and effective the original contribution that the Church has the duty of making to the welfare, the harmony, the justice and peace of these peoples. Well, there is no ecclesial Assembly if the Spirit of God is not there in the fullness of his mysterious action.

The Pope invokes him with all the fervour of his heart. May the place where the Bishops meet be a new Upper Room, much larger than the one in Jerusalem, where the Apostles were only eleven in number that morning, but, like that in Jerusalem, open to the call of the Paraclete and to the strength of a renewed Pentecost. May the Spirit accomplish in you Bishops, gathered here, the multiform mission that the Lord Jesus entrusted to him: as *interpreter of God* to make understood his plan and his word, which are inaccessible to mere human reason (cf. Jn. 14:26), may he open the understanding of the Pastors and introduce them to the Truth (cf. Jn. 16:13); *as witness of Jesus Christ,* may he give witness in their conscience and heart and transform them in turn into consistent, credible, and efficacious witnesses during their work (cf. Jn. 15:26) and put on their lips what they must say, particularly at the moment when testimony costs suffering and fatigue.

So I ask you, beloved sons and daughters, to unite with me in this Eucharist, in this invocation to the Spirit. It is not for their own sake or out of personal interest that the Bishops, from all parts of the continent, are meeting here; it is for you, People of God in these lands, and for your good. So take part in this third Conference also in this way: by asking every day for the abundance of the Holy Spirit for one and all of them.

It has been said, in a beautiful and profound way, that our God in his deepest mystery is not a solitude, but a family, since he has in himself fatherhood, sonship and the essence of the family, which is love. This subject of the family is not, therefore, extraneous to the subject of the Holy Spirit. Allow the Pope to say some words to you on this subject of the family — which will certainly occupy the Bishops during these days.

You know that the Conference of Medellín spoke of the family in pithy and urgent terms. In that year 1968, the Bishops saw, in your profound sentiment for the family, a fundamental feature of your Latin American culture. They showed that, for the good of your countries, Latin American families should always have three dimensions: education in the faith, formation of persons, promotion of development. They also emphasized the serious obstacles that families meet with in carrying out this threefold task. 'For this reason' they recommended pastoral attention for families, as one of the prior considerations of the Church in the continent.

Ten years later, the Church in Latin America feels happy at everything it has been able to do in favour of the family. But it humbly recognizes how much still remains to be done, while it perceives that the family apostolate, far from having lost its character of priority, is more urgent that ever today, as a very important element in evangelization.

The Church is aware, in fact, that the family is up against serious problems in Latin America in these times. Recently some countries have introduced divorce into their legislation, which brings a new threat to the integrity of the family. In most of your countries it is a lamentable fact that an alarming number of children, the future of these nations and the hope for the future, are born in homes without any stability or, as they are called, in 'incomplete families'. Moreover, in certain places of the 'Continent of Hope', this same hope runs the risk of vanishing, since it grows within families many of which cannot live normally owing to the particular impact upon them of the most negative effects of development: really depressing indices of unhealthiness, poverty and even want, ignorance and illiteracy, inhuman housing conditions, chronic malnutrition and so many other realities that are no less sad.

In defence of the family against these evils, the Church undertakes to give her help, and calls upon governments to take as the key point of their action an intelligent policy with regard to society and the family, a bold and persevering one, recognizing that the future — the hope — of the continent certainly lies here. It should be added that this family policy must not be understood as an indiscriminate effort to reduce the birth rate at all costs — which my predecessor Paul VI called 'reducing the number of guests at the banquet of life' — when it is well known that a balanced birth-rate is indispensable even for development. It is a question of uniting efforts to create conditions favourable to the existence of healthy and balanced families: 'to increase the food on the table', to use again an expression of Paul VI.

As well as of defence of the family, we must also speak of advancement of the family. Many organisms have to contribute to this promotion: governments and governmental organisms, the school, the trade unions, the media of social communication, groups in poor districts, the various voluntary or spontaneous associations which flourish everywhere today.

The Church must also offer her contribution in the line of her spiritual mission of proclaiming the Gospel and leading men to salvation, which also has an enormous repercussion on the welfare of the family. And what can the Church do, uniting her efforts with those of others? I am certain that your bishops will endeavour to give this question adequate, just, and efficacious answers. I point out to you how valuable is what the Church is already doing in Latin America for the family; for example: to prepare fiancés for marriage; to help families when, in the course of their existence, they go through normal crises which, if wisely guided, may even be fruitful and enriching; to make each Christian family a real 'domestic church', with all the rich content of this expression; to prepare many families for the mission of evangelizing other families; to emphasize all values of family life; to help incomplete families; to stimulate the rulers to bring forth in their countries that family social policy of which we were just speaking. The Puebla Conference will certainly support these initiatives and perhaps suggest others. We are happy to think that the history of Latin America will thus have reasons to thank the Church for all that it has done, is doing, and will do for the family in this vast continent.

Beloved sons and daughters: now, beside this altar, the Successor of Peter feels particularly close to all Latin American families. It is as if every home were to open and the Pope were able to enter into each of them; houses where there is no lack of bread or prosperity but where, perhaps, harmony and joy are lacking; houses where families live far more modestly and uncertain of the morrow, helping one another to lead a hard but dignified existence; poor houses in the suburbs of your cities, where there is much hidden suffering although there exists in the midst of them the simple gaiety of the poor: humble huts of peasants, natives, emigrants, etc. For each family in particular the Pope would like to be able to say a word of encouragement and hope. You families that can enjoy prosperity, do not shut yourselves up in your happiness; open to others to distribute what is superfluous for you and what others lack. Families oppressed by poverty, do not lose heart, and, without taking luxury as your ideal, or riches as the principle of happiness, seek with the help of all to overcome difficult moments while waiting for better days. Families visited and tormented by physical or moral pain, sorely tried by sickness or want, do not add to these sufferings bitterness or despair, but temper sorrow with hope. All families of Latin America, be sure that the Pope knows you and wishes to know you even better because he loves you with a father's tenderness

This is, in the framework of the Pope's visit to Mexico, the Day of the Family. Receive then, Latin American families, with your presence here, round the altar, by means of radio or television, receive the visit that the Pope wishes to make to each one. And give the Pope the joy of seeing you grow in the Christian values that are yours, in order that Latin America may find in its millions of families reasons to trust, to hope, to struggle and to build.

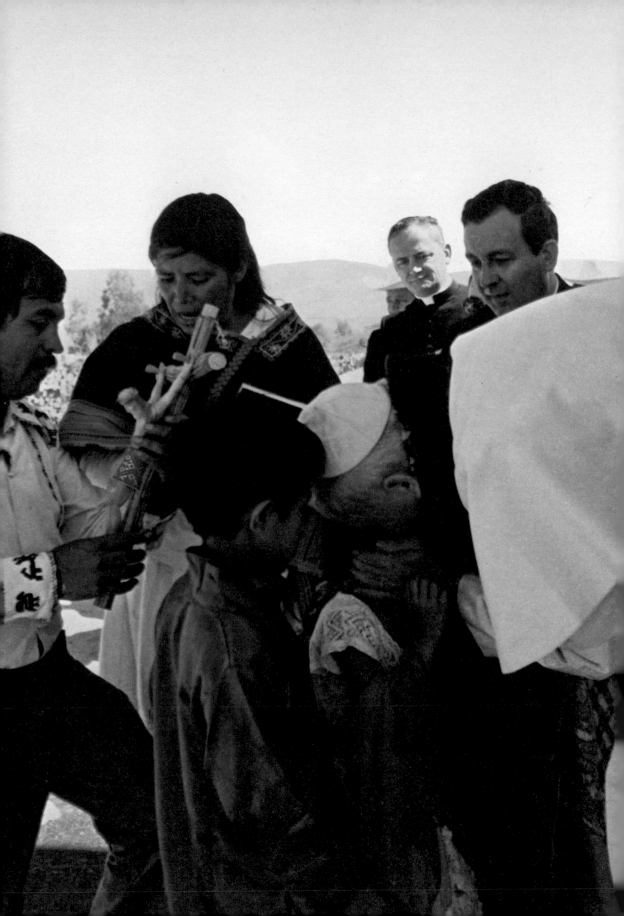

AN ECUMENICAL ENCOUNTER

In the afternoon, before starting the work
of the Third General Conference of Latin
American Bishops, John Paul II
addressed the participants in an
ecumenical gathering as follows:

Beloved Brothers in Christ,

Allow me to express to you, above all, my sincere thanks for your kindness
and for the expressions of esteem and respect that you have addressed to
me.

I wish to assure you that I, too, feel very pleased to be with you and
share this spiritual experience, feeling that Christ, our master, the Lord,
the Redeemer, Christ our hope, is in our midst. He continues to exhort us
with his pressing appeal: let them be one, Father, as you and I are one.

On my side, I said already at the beginning of my pontificate that
ecumenical concern will be one of my aims.

Let us pray, brothers, to the Lord Jesus that he may give us faithfulness
to him, faithfulness in the unity that he wished for us, in order that the
world may believe.

In order that it may be so, I call on you to recite the Our Father all
together.

POPE JOHN PAUL II's ADDRESS TO THE PUEBLA CONFERENCE

The work of the Third Conference of Latin American Bishops began at a solemn gathering in the Major Palafoxian Seminary at Puebla de Los Angeles. Pope John Paul II pronounced the opening address in the presence of all the bishops of Latin America:

Beloved Brothers in the Episcopate,

This hour that I have the happiness to experience with you is certainly an historic one for the Church in Latin America. World opinion is aware of this, as are the faithful members of your local Churches, and especially you yourselves are aware of it, you who will be the protagonists and leaders of this hour.

It is also an hour of grace, marked by the drawing near of the Lord, by a very special presence and action of the Spirit of God. For this reason we have confidently invoked that Spirit, at the beginning of our work. For this reason also I now wish to implore you, as a brother to very beloved brothers: all the days of this Conference and in every one of its acts, let yourselves be led by the Spirit, open yourselves to his inspiration and his impulse, let it be he and no other spirit that guides and strengthens you.

Under the guidance of this Spirit, for the third time in the last 25 years you, the bishops of all the countries representing the Episcopate of the Continent of Latin America, have gathered together to study more deeply together the meaning of your mission in the face of the new demands of your peoples.

The Conference that is now opening, convoked by the revered Paul VI, confirmed by my unforgettable predecessor John Paul I, and reconfirmed by

myself as one of the first acts of my pontificate, is linked with the Conference now long past, held in Rio de Janeiro, which had as its most notable result the birth of CELAM. But it is linked even more closely with the second Conference, of Medellín, of which it marks the tenth anniversary.

In these last ten years, how much progress humanity has made, and, with humanity and at its service, how much progress the Church has made! This third Conference cannot disregard that reality. It will therefore have to take as its point of departure the conclusions of Medellín, with all the positive elements that they contained, but without ignoring the incorrect interpretations at times made and which call for calm discernment, opportune criticism, and clear choices of position. You will be guided in your debates by the Working Document, prepared with such care so as to constitute the constant point of reference.

But you will also have at hand Paul VI's Apostolic Exhortation *Evangelii Nuntiandi.* With what care the great Pontiff approved as the Conference's theme: 'The present and the future of evangelization in Latin America'!

Those who were close to him during the months when the Assembly was being prepared can tell you this. They can also bear witness to the gratitude with which he learned that the basic material of the whole Conference would be this text, into which he put his whole pastoral soul, as his life drew to a close. Now that he has 'closed his eyes to this world's scene' (Testament of Paul VI), this document becomes a spiritual testament that the Conference will have to scrutinize with love and diligence, in order to make it the other obligatory point of reference, and in order to see how to put it into practice. The whole Church is grateful to you for giving, for what you are doing, and what other local Churches will perhaps do in their turn.

The Pope wishes to be with you at the beginning of your labours, and

he is thankful to the Father of lights from whom comes down every perfect gift (cf. James 1:17), for having been able to be with you at yesterday's Solemn Mass, under the maternal gaze of the Virgin of Guadalupe, as also at the Mass this morning. I would very much like to stay with you in prayer, reflection and work: be sure that I shall stay with you in spirit, while the 'anxiety for all the churches' (2 Cor. 11:28) calls me elsewhere. I wish at least, before continuing my pastoral visit through Mexico and before my return to Rome, to leave you as a pledge of my spiritual presence a few words, uttered with the solicitous care of a Pastor and the affection of a Father; words which are the echo of my main preoccupations regarding the theme you have to deal with and regarding the life of the Church in these beloved countries.

TEACHERS OF TRUTH

It is a great consolation for the universal Father to note that you come together here not as a symposium of experts, not as a parliament of politicians, not as a congress of scientists or technologists, however important such assemblies may be, but as a fraternal encounter of Pastors of the Church. And as Pastors you have the vivid awareness that your principal duty is to be Teachers of the Truth. Not a human and rational truth, but the Truth that comes from God, the Truth that brings with it the principle of the authentic liberation of man: 'you will know the truth, and the truth will make you free' (Jn. 8:32); that Truth which is the only one that offers a solid basis for an adequate 'praxis'.

I. 1 To be watchful for purity of doctrine, the basis in building up the Christian community, is therefore, together with the proclamation of the Gospel, the primary and irreplaceable duty of the pastor, of the Teacher of the faith. How often Saint Paul emphasized this, convinced as he was of the seriousness of the accomplishment of this duty (cf. 1 Tim. 1:3–7; 18–20; 4:11, 16; 2 Tim. 1:4–14). Over and above unity in love, unity in truth is always urgent for us. The beloved Pope Paul VI, in the Apostolic Exhortation *Evangelii Nuntiandi,* said: 'The Gospel entrusted to us is also the word of truth. A truth which liberates and which alone gives peace of heart is what people are looking for when we proclaim the Good News to them. The truth about God, about man and his mysterious destiny, about the world . . . The preacher of the Gospel will therefore be a person who even at the price of personal renunciation and suffering always seeks the truth that he must transmit to others. He never betrays or hides truth out of a desire to please men, in order to astonish or to shock, nor for the sake of originality or a desire to make an impression . . . We are the pastors of the faithful people, and our pastoral service impels us to preserve, defend, and to communicate the truth regardless of the sacrifices that this involves' (*Evangelii Nuntiandi,* 78).

I.2 From you, Pastors, the faithful of your countries expect and demand above all a careful and zealous transmission of the truth concerning Jesus

Christ. This truth is at the centre of evangelization and constitutes its essential content: 'There is no true evangelization if the name, the teaching, the life, the promises, the Kingdom and the mystery of Jesus of Nazareth, the Son of God are not proclaimed' *(Evangelii Nuntiandi,* 22).

From the living knowledge of this truth will depend the vigour of the faith of millions of people. From it will also depend the strength of their support of the Church and of their active presence as Christians in the world. From this knowledge there will derive choices, values, attitudes and modes of behaviour capable of orienting and defining our Christian life and of creating new people, and hence a new humanity, for the conversion of the individual and social conscience (cf. *Evangelii Nuntiandi,* 18).

It is from a solid Christology that there must come light on so many doctrinal and pastoral themes and questions that you intend to study in these coming days.

I.3 And then we have to confess Christ before history and the world with a conviction that is profound, deeply felt and lived, just as Peter confessed him: 'You are the Christ the Son of the living God.' (Mt. 16:16.)

This is the Good News in a certain sense unique: the Church lives by it and for it, just as she draws from it everything that she has to offer to people, without any distinction of nation, culture, race, time, age or condition. For this reason 'from that confession of faith (Peter's) the sacred history of salvation and of the People of God could not fail to take on a new dimension' (Homily of Pope John Paul II at the solemn inauguration of his Pontificate, 22 October 1978).

This is the one Gospel, and 'even if we, or an angel from heaven, should preach to you a gospel contrary to that which we preached to you, let him be accursed', as the Apostle wrote in very clear terms (Gal. 1:8).

I.4 In fact, today there occur in many places — the phenomenon is not a new one — 're-readings' of the Gospel, the result of theoretical speculations rather than authentic meditation on the word of God and a true commitment to the Gospel. They cause confusion by diverging from the central criteria of the faith of the Church, and some people have the temerity to pass them on, under the guise of catechesis, to the Christian communities.

In some cases either Christ's divinity is passed over in silence, or some people in fact fall into forms of interpretation at variance with the Church's faith. Christ is said to be merely a 'prophet', one who proclaimed God's Kingdom and love, but not the true Son of God, and therefore not the centre and object of the very Gospel message.

In other cases people claim to show Jesus as politically committed, as one who fought against Roman oppression and the authorities, and also as one involved in the class struggle. The idea of Christ as a political figure, a revolutionary, as the subversive man from Nazareth, does not tally with the Church's catechesis. By confusing the insidious pretexts of Jesus' accusers with the — very different — attitude of Jesus himself, some people adduce as

the cause of his death the outcome of a political conflict, and nothing is said of the Lord's will to deliver himself and of his consciousness of his redemptive mission. The Gospels clearly show that for Jesus anything that would alter his mission as the Servant of Yahweh was a temptation (cf. Mt. 4:8; Lk. 4:5). He does not accept the position of those who mixed the things of God with merely political attitudes (cf. Mt. 22:21; Mk. 12:17; Jn. 18:36). He unequivocally rejects recourse to violence. He opens his message of conversion to everybody, without excluding the very Publicans. The perspective of his mission is much deeper. It consists in complete salvation through a transforming, peacemaking, pardoning and reconciling love. There is no doubt, moreover, that all this is very demanding for the attitude of the Christian who wishes truly to serve his least brethren, the poor, the needy, the emarginated; in a word, all those who in their lives reflect the sorrowing face of the Lord (cf. *Lumen Gentium*, 8).

I.5. Against such 're-readings' therefore, and against the perhaps brilliant but fragile and inconsistent hypotheses flowing from them, 'Evangelization in the present and future of Latin America' cannot cease to affirm the Church's faith: Jesus Christ, the Word and the Son of God, becomes man in order to come close to man and to offer him, through the power of his mystery, salvation, the great gift of God (cf. *Evangelii Nuntiandi,* 19 and 27).

This is the faith that has permeated your history and has formed the best of the values of your peoples and must go on animating, with every energy, the dynamism of their future. This is the faith that reveals the vocation to harmony and unity that must drive away the dangers of war in this continent of hope, in which the Church has been such a powerful factor of integration. This is the faith, finally, which the faithful people of Latin America through their religious practices and popular piety express with such vitality and in such varied ways.

From this faith in Christ, from the bosom of the Church, we are able to serve men and women, our peoples, and to penetrate their culture with the Gospel, to transform hearts, and to make systems and structures more human.

Any form of silence, disregard, mutilation or inadequate emphasis of the whole of the Mystery of Jesus Christ that diverges from the Church's faith cannot be the valid content of evangelization. 'Today, under the pretext of a piety that is false, under the deceptive appearance of a preaching of the Gospel, some people are trying to deny the Lord Jesus', wrote a great Bishop in the midst of the hard crises of the fourth century. And he added: 'I speak the truth, so that the cause of the confusion that we are suffering may be known to all. I cannot keep silent' (Saint Hilary of Poitiers, *Contra Auxentium,* 1–4). Nor can you, the bishops of today, keep silent when this confusion occurs.

This is what Pope Paul VI recommended in his opening discourse at the Medellín Conference: 'Talk, speak out, preach, write. United in purpose and in programme, defend and explain the truths of the faith by taking a position on the present validity of the Gospel, on questions dealing with the life of the faithful and the defence of Christian conduct . . .' (Pope Paul VI's Discourse, I).

I too will not grow weary of repeating, as my duty of evangelizing the whole of mankind obliges me to do: 'Do not be afraid. Open wide the doors for Christ. To his saving power open the boundaries of States, economic and political systems, the vast fields of culture, civilization and development' (the Pope's Homily at the Inauguration of the Pontificate, 22 October 1978).

I.6. You are teachers of the Truth, and you are expected to proclaim unceasingly, but with the special vigour at this moment, the truth concerning the mission of the Church, object of the Creed that we profess, and an indispensable and fundamental area of our fidelity. The Church was established by the Lord as a fellowship of life, love and truth *(Lumen Gentium,* 9) and as the body, the *Pleroma* and the sacrament of Christ, in whom the whole fullness of deity dwells *(Lumen Gentium,* 7).

The Church is born of our response in faith to Christ. In fact, it is by sincere acceptance of the Good News that we believers gather together in Jesus' name in order to seek together the Kingdom, build it up and live it (cf. *Evangelii Nuntiandi,* 13). The Church is 'the assembly of those who in faith look to Jesus as the cause of salvation and the source of unity and peace' *(Lumen Gentium,* 9).

But on the other hand we are born of the Church. She communicates to us the riches of life and grace entrusted to her. She generates us by baptism, feeds us with the sacraments and the word of God, prepares us for mission, leads us to God's plan, the reason for our existence as Christians. We are her children. With just pride we call her our Mother, repeating a title coming down from the centuries, from the earliest times (cf. Henri de Lubac, *Méditation sur l'Eglise).*

She must therefore be called upon, respected and served, for 'one cannot have God for his Father, if he does not have the Church for his Mother' (Saint Cyprian, *De Unitate,* 6, 8), one cannot love Christ without loving the Church which Christ loves (cf. *Evangelii Nuntiandi,* 16), and 'to extent that one loves the Church of Christ, he possesses the Holy Spirit' (Saint Augustine, *In Ioannem tract.,* 32, 8).

Love for the Church must be composed of fidelity and trust. Stressing, in the first discourse of my pontificate, my resolve to be faithful to the Second Vatican Council and my desire to dedicate my greatest care to the ecclesiological area, I called on people to take once again into their hands the Dogmatic Constitution *Lumen Gentium* in order to 'meditate with renewed and invigorating zeal on the nature and function of the Church, her way of being and acting . . . not merely in order that the vital communion in Christ of all who believe and hope in him should be accomplished, but also in order to contribute to bringing about a fuller and closer unity of the whole human family' (First Message of John Paul II to the Church and the World, 17 October 1978).

Now, at this surpassing moment in the evangelization of Latin America, I repeat the call: 'Assent to this document of the Council, seen in the light of Tradition and embodying the dogmatic formulae issued a century ago by the First Vatican Council, will be for us, pastors and faithful, a clear signpost and urgent incentive for walking – let us repeat – the paths of life and history' (*ibid.*).

I.7. There is no guarantee of serious and vigorous evangelizing activity without a well-founded ecclesiology.

The first reason is that evangelization is the essential mission, the distinctive vocation and the deepest identity of the Church, which has in turn been evangelized (*Evangelii Nuntiandi*, 14–15; *Lumen Gentium*, 5). She has been sent by the Lord and in her turn sends evangelizers to preach 'not their own selves or their personal ideas, but a Gospel of which neither she nor they are the absolute masters and owners, to dispose of it as they wish' (*Evangelii Nuntiandi*, 15). A second reason is that 'evangelization is for no one an individual and isolated act; it is one that is deeply ecclesial (*Evangelii Nuntiandi*, 60), which is not subject to the discretionary power of individualistic criteria and perspectives but to that of communion with the Church and her pastors (cf. *ibid.*).

How could there be authentic evangelizing, if there were no ready and sincere reverence for the sacred Magisterium, in clear awareness that by submitting to it the People of God are not accepting the word of men but the true word of God? (cf. 1 Thess. 2:13; *Lumen Gentium*, 12). 'The "objective" importance of this Magisterium must always be kept in mind and also safeguarded, because of the attacks being levelled nowadays in various quarters against some certain truths of the Catholic faith' (First Message of John Paul II to the Church and the World, 17 October 1978).

I well know your attachment and availability to the See of Peter and the love that you have always shown it. From my heart I thank you in the Lord's name for the deeply ecclesial attitude implied in this and I wish you yourselves the consolation of counting on the loyal attachment of your faithful.

I.8. In the abundant documentation with which you have prepared this Conference, especially in the contributions of many Churches, a certain uneasiness is at times noticed with regard to the very interpretation of the nature and mission of the Church. Allusion is made, for instance, to the separation that some set up between the Church and the Kingdom of God. The Kingdom of God is emptied of its full content and is understood in a rather secularist sense: it is interpreted as being reached not by faith and membership in the Church but by the mere changing of structures and social and political involvement and activity for justice. This is to forget that 'the Church receives the mission to proclaim and to establish among all peoples the Kingdom of Christ and of God. She becomes on earth the seed and beginning of that Kingdom' (*Lumen Gentium*, 5).

In one of his beautiful catechetical instructions Pope John Paul I, speaking of the virtue of hope, warned that 'it is wrong to state that political, economic and social liberation coincides with salvation in Jesus Christ, that the *Regnum Dei* is identified with the *Regnum hominis'*.

In some cases an attitude of mistrust is produced with regard to the 'institutional' or 'official' Church, which is considered as alienating, as opposed to another Church of the people, one 'springing from the people and taking concrete form in the poor. These positions could contain different, not always easily measured, degrees of familiar ideological forms of conditioning. The Council has reminded us what is the nature and mission of the Church. It has reminded us how her profound unity and permanent up-building are contributed to by those who are responsible for the ministry of the community and have to count on the collaboration of the whole People of God. In fact, 'if the Gospel that we proclaim is seen to be rent by doctrinal disputes, ideological polarizations or mutual condemnations among Christians, at the mercy of the latter's differing views on Christ and the Church and even because of their different concepts of society and human institutions, how can those to whom we address our preaching fail to be disturbed, disoriented, even scandalized?' (*Evangelii Nuntiandi,* 77).

I.9. The truth that we owe to man is, first and foremost, a truth about man. As witnesses of Jesus Christ we are heralds, spokesmen and servants of this truth. We cannot reduce it to the principles of a system of philosophy or to pure political activity. We cannot forget it or betray it.

Perhaps one of the most obvious weaknesses of present-day civilization lies in an inadequate view of man. Without doubt, our age is the one in which man has been most written and spoken of, the age of the forms of humanism and the age of anthropocentrism. Nevertheless it is paradoxically also the age of man's abasement to previously unsuspected levels, the age of human values trampled on as never before.

How is this paradox explained? We can say that it is the inexorable paradox of atheistic humanism. It is the drama of man being deprived of an essential dimension of his being, namely, his search for the infinite, and thus faced with having his being reduced in the worst way. The Pastoral Constitution *Gaudium et Spes* plumbs the depths of the problem when it says: 'Only in the mystery of the Incarnate Word does the mystery of man take on light' (*Gaudium et Spes,* 22).

Thanks to the Gospel, the Church has the truth about man. This truth is found in an anthropology that the Church never ceases to fathom more thoroughly and to communicate to others. The primordial affirmation of this anthropology is that man is God's image and cannot be reduced to a mere portion of nature or a nameless element in the human city (cf. *Gaudium et Spes,* 12 and 14). This is the meaning of what Saint Irenaeus wrote: 'Man's glory is God, but the recipient of God's every action, of his wisdom and of his power is man' (Saint Irenaeus, *Adversus Haereses,* III, 20, 2–3).

I made particular reference to this irreplaceable foundation of the

74

Christian concept of man in my Christmas Message: 'Christmas is the feast of man . . . Man is an object to be counted, something considered under the aspect of quantity . . . Yet at the same time he is a single being, unique and unrepeatable . . . somebody thought of and chosen from eternity, someone called and identified by his own name' (Christmas Message, 1).

Faced with so many other forms of humanism that are often shut in by a strictly economic, biological or psychological view of man, the Church has the right and the duty to proclaim the Truth about man that she received from her teacher, Jesus Christ. God grant that no external compulsion may prevent her from doing so. God grant, above all, that she may not cease to do so through fear or doubt, through having let herself be contaminated by other forms of humanism, or through lack of confidence in her original message.

When a Pastor of the Church proclaims clearly and unambiguously the Truth about man that was revealed by him who 'knew what was in man' (Jn. 2:25), he must therefore be encouraged by the certainty of doing the best service to the human being.

The complete truth about the human being constitutes the foundation of the Church's social teaching and the basis also of true liberation. In the light of this truth, man is not a being subjected to economic or political processes; these processes are instead directed to man and are subjected to him.

Without doubt, this truth about man that the Church teaches will go out strengthened from this meeting of Pastors.

BUILDERS OF UNITY

Your pastoral, service of truth is completed by a like service of unity.

II.1 Unity among Bishops

Unity will be, first of all, unity among yourselves, the Bishops. 'We must guard and keep this unity,' the Bishop Saint Cyprian wrote in a moment of grave threats to communion between the Bishops of his country, 'especially we Bishops who preside over the Church, in order to give witness that the Episcopate is one and indivisible. Let no one mislead the faithful or alter the truth. The Episcopate is one' (*De Ecclesiae Catholicae Unitate*, 6–8).

This unity of Bishops comes not from human calculations and strategy but from on high: from serving one Lord, from being animated by one Spirit, and from loving one and the same Church. It is unity resulting from the mission that Christ has entrusted to us, the mission that has been evolving on the Latin American continent for almost half a millenium, and that you are carrying forward with stout hearts in times of profound changes as we approach the close of the second millennium of redemption and of the Church's activity. It is unity around the Gospel, the Body and Blood of the Lamb, and Peter living in his Successors; all of which are different signs, but all of them highly important signs, of the presence of Jesus among us.

What an occasion you have, dear Brothers, for living this unity of Pastors in this Conference! In itself it is a sign and result of an already existing unity; but it is also an anticipation and beginning of a unity that must be more and more close and solid. Begin your work in a climate of brotherly unity: even now let this unity be a component of evangelization.

II.2. Unity with priests, religious and faithful

Let unity among the Bishops be extended by unity with priests, religious and faithful. Priests are the immediate collaborators of the Bishops in their pastoral mission, and their mission would be compromised if close unity did not reign between priests and Bishops.

Men and women religious are also especially important subjects of that unity. I well know the importance of their contribution to evangelization in Latin America in the past and in the present. They came here at the dawn of the discovery and accompanied the first steps of almost all the countries. They worked continuously here together with the diocesan clergy. In some countries more than half, in other countries the great majority, of the body of priests are religious. This would be enough to show how important it is here more than in other parts of the world for religious not only to accept but to seek loyally an unbreakable unity of aim and action with their Bishops. To the Bishops the Lord entrusted the mission of feeding the flock. To religious it belongs to blaze the trails for evangelization. It cannot be, it ought not to be, that the Bishops should lack the responsible and active, yet at the same time, docile and trusting collaboration of the religious, whose charism makes them ever more ready agents at the service of the Gospel. In this matter everybody in the ecclesial community has the duty of avoiding magisteria other than the Church's Magisterium, for they are ecclesially unacceptable and pastorally sterile.

The laity also are subjects of that unity, whether involved individually or joined in apostolic associations for the spreading of the Kingdom of God. It is they who have to consecrate the world to Christ in the midst of their daily duties and in their various family and professional tasks, in close union with and obedience to the lawful Pastors.

In line with *Lumen Gentium*, we must safeguard the precious gift of ecclesial unity between all those who form part of the pilgrim People of God.

DEFENDERS AND PROMOTERS OF HUMAN DIGNITY

III. 1. Those familiar with the Church's history know that in all periods there have been admirable Bishops deeply involved in advancing and valiantly defending the human dignity of those entrusted to them by the Lord. They have always been impelled to do so by their episcopal mission, because they considered human dignity a Gospel value that cannot be despised without greatly offending the Creator.

This dignity is infringed on the individual level when due regard is not had for values such as freedom, the right to profess one's religion, physical and mental integrity, the right to essential goods, to life . . . It is infringed on the social and political level when man cannot exercise his right of participation, or when he is subjected to unjust and unlawful coercion, or submitted to physical or mental torture, etc.

I am not unaware of how many questions are being posed in this sphere today in Latin America. As Bishops, you cannot fail to concern yourselves with them. I know that you propose to carry out a serious reflection on the relationships and implications between evangelization and human advancement or liberation, taking into consideration, in such a vast and important field, what is specific about the Church's presence.

Here is where we find, brought concretely into practice, the themes we have touched upon in speaking of the truth concerning Christ, the Church and man.

III.2. If the Church makes herself present in the defence of, or in the advancement of, man, she does so in line with her mission, which, although it is religious and not social or political, cannot fail to consider man in the entirety of his being. The Lord outlined in the parable of the Good Samaritan the model of attention to all human needs (cf. Lk. 10:29ff.), and he said that in the final analysis he will identify himself with the disinherited – the sick, the imprisoned, the hungry, the lonely – who have been given a helping hand (Mt. 25:31ff). The Church has learned in these and other pages of the Gospel (cf. Mk. 6 :35–44) that the evangelizing mission has, as an essential part, action for justice and the tasks of the advancement of man (cf. final document of the Synod of Bishops, October 1971), and that between evangelization and human advancement there are very strong links of the orders of anthropology, theology and love (cf. *Evangelii Nuntiandi,* 31); so that 'evangelization would not be complete if it did not take into account the unceasing interplay of the Gospel and of man's concrete life, both personal and social' *(Evangelii Nuntiandi*, 29).

Let us also keep in mind that the Church's action in earthly matters such as human advancement, development, justice, the rights of the individual, is always intended to be at the service of man; and of man as she sees him in the Christian vision of the anthropology that she adopts. She therefore does not need to have recourse to ideological systems in order to love, defend and collaborate in the liberation of man: at the centre of the message of which she is the depositary and herald she finds inspiration for acting in favour of brotherhood, justice, and peace, against all forms of domination, slavery, discrimination, violence, attacks on religious liberty and aggression against man, and whatever attacks life (cf. *Gaudium et Spes,* 26, 27 and 29).

III.3 It is therefore not through opportunism nor thirst for novelty that the Church, 'the expert in humanity' (Paul VI, Address to the United Nations, 4 October 1965) defends human rights. It is through a true *evangelical commitment*, which, as happened with Christ, is a commitment to the most needy. In fidelity to this commitment, the Church wishes to stay free with regard to the competing systems, in order to opt only for man. Whatever the miseries or sufferings that afflict man, it is not through violence, the interplay of power and political systems, but through the truth concerning man, that he journeys towards a better future.

III.4. Hence the Church's constant preoccupation with the delicate question of property. A proof of this is the writings of the Fathers of the Church through the first thousand years of Christianity (cf. St Ambrose, *De Nabuthe,* c. 12, n. 53: *PL* 14, 747). It is clearly shown by the vigorous teaching of Saint Thomas Aquinas, repeated so many times. In our own times, the Church has appealed to the same principles in such far-reaching documents as the social Encyclicals of the recent Popes. With special force and profundity, Pope Paul VI spoke of this subject in his Encyclical *Populorum Progressio* (cf. nos. 23–24; cf. also *Mater et Magistra,* 1.06).

This voice of the Church, echoing the voice of human conscience, and which did not cease to make itself heard down the centuries in the midst of the most varied social and cultural systems and conditions, deserves and needs to be heard in our time also, when the growing wealth of a few parallels the growing poverty of the masses.

It is then that the Church's teaching, according to which all private property involves a social obligation, acquires an urgent character. With respect to this teaching, the Church has a mission to carry out; she must preach, educate individuals and collectivites, form public opinion, and offer orientations to the leaders of the peoples. In this way she will be working in favour of society, within which this Christian and evangelical principle will finally bear the fruit of a more just and equitable distribution of goods, not only within each nation but also in the world in general, ensuring that the stronger countries do not use their power to the detriment of the weaker ones.

Those who bear responsibility for the public life of the States and nations will have to understand that internal peace and international peace can only be ensured if a social and economic system based on justice flourishes.

Christ did not remain indifferent in the face of this vast and demanding imperative of social morality. Nor could the Church. In the spirit of the Church, which is the spirit of Christ, and relying upon her ample and solid doctrine, let us return to work in this field.

It must be emphasized here once more that the Church's solicitude looks to the whole man.

For this reason, for an economic system to be just it is an indispensable condition that it should favour the development and diffusion of public education and culture. The more just the economy, the deeper will be the conscience of culture. This is very much in line with what the Council stated: that to attain a life worthy of man, it is not possible to limit oneself to *having more;* one must aspire to *being more* (cf. *Gaudium et Spes,* 35).

Therefore, Brothers, drink at these authentic fountains. Speak with the language of the Council, of John XXIII, of Paul VI: it is the language of the experience, of the suffering, of the hope of modern humanity.

When Paul VI declared that development is 'the new name of peace' (*Populorum Progressio,* 76). he had in mind all the links of interdependence that exist not only within the nations but also those outside them, on the world level. He took into consideration the mechanisms that, because they happen to be imbued not with authentic humanism but with materialism, produce on the international level rich people ever more rich at the expense of poor people ever more poor.

There is no economic rule capable of changing these mechanisms by itself. It is necessary, in international life, to call upon ethical principles, the demands of justice, the primary commandment which is that of love. Primacy must be given to what is moral, to what is spiritual, to what springs from the full truth concerning man.

I have wished to manifest to you these reflections which I consider very important, although they must not distract you from the central theme of the Conference: we shall reach man, we shall reach justice, through evangelization.

III.5. In the face of what has been said hitherto, the Church sees with deep sorrow 'the sometimes massive increase of human rights violations in all parts of society and of the world . . . Who can deny that today individual persons and civil powers violate basic rights of the human person with impunity: rights such as the right to be born, the right to life, the right to responsible procreation, to work, to peace, to freedom and social justice, the right to participate in the decisions that affect people and nations? And what can be said when we face the various forms of collective violence like discrimination against individuals and groups, the use of physical and psychological torture perpetrated against prisoners or political dissenters? The list grows when we turn to the instances of the abduction of persons for political reasons and look at the acts of kidnapping for material gain which attack so dramatically family life and the social fabric' (Message of John Paul II to the Secretary-General of the United Nations Organization on 2 December 1978: 30th Anniversary of the Declaration of Human Rights). We cry out once more: Respect man! He is the image of God! Evangelize, so that this may become a reality; so that the Lord may transform hearts and humanize the political and economic systems, with man's responsible commitment as the starting point!

III.6. Pastoral commitments in this field must be encouraged through a correct Christian idea of liberation. The Church feels the duty to proclaim the liberation of millions of human beings, the duty to help this liberation become firmly established (cf. *Evangelii Nuntiandi*, 30); but she also feels the corresponding duty to proclaim liberation in its integral and profound meaning, as Jesus proclaimed and realized it (cf. *Evangelii Nuntiandi*, 31). 'Liberation from everything that oppresses man but which is, above all, liberation from sin and the Evil One, in the joy of knowing God and being known by him' (*Evangelii Nuntiandi*, 9). Liberation made up of reconciliation and forgiveness. Lieberation springing from the reality of being children of God, whom we are able to call Abba, Father (Rom. 8:15); a reality which makes us recognize in every man a brother of ours, capable of being transformed in his heart through God's mercy. Liberation that, with the energy of love, urges us towards fellowship, the summit and fullness of which we find in the Lord. Liberation as the overcoming of the various forms of slavery and man-made idols, and as the growth of the new man. Liberation that in the framework of the Church's proper mission is not reduced to the simple and narrow economic, political, social or cultural dimension, and is not sacrificed to the demands of any strategy, practice or short term solution (cf. *Evangelii Nuntiandi*, 33).

To safeguard the originality of Christian liberation and the energies that it is capable of releasing, one must at all costs avoid any form of curtailment or ambiguity, as Pope Paul VI asked: 'The Church would lose her fundamental meaning. Her message of liberation would no longer have any originality and would easily be open to monopolization and manipulation by ideological systems and political parties' (*Evangelii Nuntiandi*, 32). There are many signs that help to distinguish when the liberation in question is Christian and when on the other hand it is based rather on ideologies that rob it of consistency with an evangelical view of man, of things and of events (cf. *Evangelii Nuntiandi*, 35). They are signs drawn from the content of what the evangelizers proclaim or from the concrete attitudes that they adopt. At the level of content, one must see what is their fidelity to the word of God, to the Church's living Tradition and to her Magisterium. As for attitudes, one must consider what sense of communion they have with the Bishops, in the first place, and with the other sectors of the People of God; what contribution they make to the real building up of the community; in what form they lovingly show care for the poor, the sick, the dispossessed, the neglected and the oppressed, and in what way they find in them the image of the poor and suffering Jesus, and strive to relieve their need and serve Christ in them (cf. *Lumen Gentium*, 8). Let us not deceive ourselves: the humble and simple faithful, as though by an evangelical instinct, spontaneously sense when the Gospel is served in the Church and when it is emptied of its content and is stifled with other interests.

As you see, the series of observations made by *Evangelii Nuntiandi* on the theme of liberation retains all its validity.

III.7. What we have already recalled constitutes a rich and complex heritage, which *Evangelii Nuntiandi* calls the Social Doctrine or Social Teaching of the Church (cf. *Evangelii Nuntiandi,* 38). This teaching comes into being, in the light of the Word of God and the authentic Magisterium, from the presence of Christians in the midst of the changing situations of the world, in contact with the challenges that result from those situations. This social doctrine involves therefore both principles for reflection and also norms for judgment and guidelines for action (cf. *Octogesima Adveniens,* 4).

Placing responsible confidence in this social doctrine — even though some people seek to sow doubts and lack of confidence in it — to give it serious study, to try to apply it, to teach it, to be faithful to it: all this is the guarantee, in a member of the Church, of his commitment in the delicate and demanding social tasks, and of his efforts in favour of the liberation or advancement of his brothers and sisters.

Allow me therefore to recommend to your special pastoral attention the urgent need to make your faithful people aware of this social doctrine of the Church.

Particular care must be given to forming a social conscience at all levels and and in all sectors. When injustices grow worse and the distance between rich and poor increases distressingly, the social doctrine, in a form which is creative and open to the broad fields of the Church's presence, must be a valuable instrument for formation and action. This holds good particularly for the laity: 'it is to the laity, though not exclusively to them, that secular duties and activity properly belong' (*Gaudium et Spes,* 43). It is necessary to avoid supplanting the laity and to study seriously just when certain forms of supplying for them retain their reason for existence. Is it not the laity who are called, by reason of their vocation in the Church, to make their contribution in the political and economic dimensions, and to be effectively present in the safe-guarding and advancement of human rights?

You are going to consider many pastoral themes of great significance. Time prevents me from mentioning them. Some I have referred to or will do so in the meetings with the priests, religious, seminarians and lay people.

SOME PRIORITY TASKS

IV.1. The themes that I indicate here have, for different reasons, great importance. You will not fail to consider them, among the many others that your pastoral farsightedness will indicate to you.

a) The Family: Make every effort to ensure that there is pastoral care for the family. Attend to this field of such primary importance in the certainty that evangelization in the future depends largely on the 'domestic Church'. It is the school of love, of the knowledge of God, of respect for life and for human dignity. The importance of this pastoral care is in proportion to the threats aimed at the family. Think of the campaigns in favour of divorce, of the use of contraceptive practices, and of abortion, which destroy society.

b) Priestly and religious vocations: In the majority of your countries, in spite of an encouraging awakening of vocations, the lack of vocations is a grave and chronic problem. There is a huge disproportion between the growing population and the number of agents of evangelization. This is of great importance to the Christian community. Every community has to obtain its vocations, as a sign of it vitality and maturity. Intense pastoral activity must be reactivated, starting with the Christian vocation in general and from enthusiastic pastoral care for youth, so as to give the Church the ministers she needs. Lay vocations, although they are so indispensable, cannot compensate for them. Furthermore, one of the proofs of the laity's commitment is an abundance of vocations to the consecrated life.

c) Youth: How much hope the Church places in youth! How much energy needed by the Church abounds in youth, in Latin America! How close we Pastors must be to the young, so that Christ and the Church and love of the brethren may penetrate deeply into their hearts.

At the end of this message I cannot fail to invoke once again the protection of the Mother of God upon your persons and your work during these days. The fact that this meeting of ours is taking place in the spiritual presence of Our Lady of Guadalupe, who is venerated in Mexico and in all the other countries as the Mother of the Church in Latin America, is for me a cause of joy and a source of hope. May she, the 'Star of evangelization', be your guide in your future reflections and decisions. May she obtain for you from her Divine Son:
    — the boldness of prophets and the evangelical prudence of Pastors,
    — the clearsightedness of teachers and the reliability of guides and directors,
    — courage as witnesses, and the calmness, patience and gentleness of fathers.

May the Lord bless your labours. You are accompanied by select representatives: priests, deacons, men and women religious, lay people, experts and observers, whose collaboration will be very useful to you. The whole Church has its eyes on you, with confidence and hope. You intend to respond to these expectations with full fidelity to Christ, the Church, and humanity. The future is in God's hands, but in a certain way God places that future with new evangelizing momentum in your hands too. 'Go therefore and make disciples of all nations.' (Mt. 28:19.)

You are the Voice
of the Silent

Monday 29 January

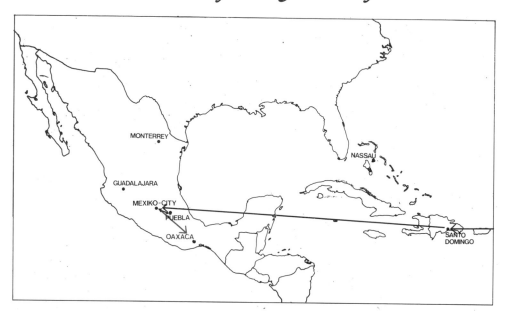

WITH THE SICK CHILDREN

The fourth day of the Pope in Mexico began with what had become a customary awakening by one or other of the picturesque small choirs with the addition, on that morning, of a group of girls in local costume. John Paul II went down to greet them before setting off in the presidential helicopter for the Children's Hospital in Mexico City. During this journey the Pope flew at low level, and blessed, the suburb of Santa Fé, on the southern outskirts of the capital, where fifty thousand people live in great poverty. The village called 'Paz y Alegria' (Peace and Joy) is in the area. Then onward to the hospital. There was a moving scene when 314 seriously ill children welcomed the Pope with delight.

Pope John Paul II visited the departments of neurosurgery and orthopaedics. Perhaps the most touching encounter was with those children affected by congenital, and more or less incurable, diseases, against which the doctors are fighting with little hope of success. John Paul II was deeply moved, and comforted the small sufferers, enquiring about their condition and speaking words of hope to each one. In a brief talk to all those present, both doctors and patients, the Pope promised to pray frequently for the sick vhildren and asked them all to join him in saying an Ave Maria to the Virgin of Guadalupe.

Beloved Children,

On coming to spend these moments in your midst, I wish to greet the directors of the Centre, all the sick boys and girls in this Children's Hospital, and all the children who are suffering in their homes, in any part of Mexico.

Sickness prevents you from playing with your friends; so another friend, the Pope, who thinks of you so often and prays for you, has desired to come and see you.

I also greet your parents, brothers, sisters, relatives and all those who are concerned about your health and care for you with such attention and affection.

I now call on you to recite a Hail Mary to the Virgin of Guadalupe for you, who meet pain and sickness so early in your lives.

Beloved children, the Pope will continue to remember you and he takes with him your smiling greeting with open arms, leaving you his embrace and his Blessing.

THE FLIGHT TO OAXACA

The plane which carried the Holy Father and his suite from Mexico City took off at 10.33 a.m. After a few minutes in flight, the Captain of the Mexican Air Lines Boeing 727, wanted, like so many others, to pay his respects to the Pope and spoke to him in Polish on the intercom. Oaxaca is only five hundred kilometres from Mexico City, and the Boeing took a mere thirty-five minutes to complete the journey after flying over the volcanic area dominated by the 5400 metre high Popocatepetl, the highest peak in Mexico, as well as the picturesque mountain of Iztaccihuatl.

A big crowd of Indians, wearing their traditional Zapotec costume, were waiting at the Benito Juarez Airport at Oaxaca to greet the Pope. As he walked by, a group of these in native costume, surmounted by marvellous hats like haloes, made of plumes of the quetzal bird with white and yellow pennants on top, executed the dance of the feathers on a small stage which had been erected close to the landing area.

The Holy Father was then received by Monsignor Bartolomé Carrasco, the Archbishop of Oaxaca, who made a speech of welcome, to which the Pope replied as follows:

Lord Archbishop,

Beloved Brothers and Sons,

Many thanks to you all for the cordial reception you have given me on my arrival at this land of Oaxaca. Many thanks, too, to the Lord Archbishop for his words of welcome.

I am overcome with emotion and grateful wonder at seeing with what affability, with what enthusiasm, you welcome me in your midst: a sign beyond all doubt that you have always felt very close in affection to the Vicar of Christ, the Pastor of the universal Church and, therefore, yours also.

At this first meeting with you, I wish only to express to you my deep respect and appreciation for this land of Oaxaca, rich in history, traditions, and religious spirit; the cradle, furthermore, of various peoples that are natives of this area who have left an indelible mark on Mexican history. Peoples and men who have bequeathed to you something that you cultivate as a real heritage: deep esteem for moral and spiritual values.

I also greet very cordially those who were unable to come here, particularly the sick and the old. To all of them and to you, my fullest Blessing.

WITH THE INDIANS OF CUILAPAN

John Paul II climbed into a helicopter to visit the town of Cuilapan where eighty per cent of the Mixtec population lives. Here the Pope came into contact with the most basic and depressing reality of Mexican society. Through the individuality of their folklore, the Indians of Cuilapan proved to the Pope their ethnic variety. These 350,000 people belong to more than thirty tribes, not merely distinct from one another but actually unable to communicate because each tribe, or at least the great majority, is only able to speak its own dialect. John Paul II conversed with them for an hour and a half, a short but an unforgettable meeting, hard to describe. It is difficult to give the atmosphere of such an unusual and moving encounter.

'Trabauroka erhuitn chet ndian — we suffer a great deal; we are without work. It is Esteban speaking, aged forty-eight, married with seven children who, in front of the ruins of the former convent of the Capuchins, salutes the Pope on behalf of the 100,000 and more Indians living in this area. Esteban is an Indian of Zapotec origin, and he could only speak his own dialect, but he made himself understood because the deeper meaning of what he was saying was delineated in a thousand faces around him, whose smiles and pleasure in that very special moment, barely concealed a condition quite unworthy of human beings.

'Datu gunibatu eneuda pekte ki betua — I salute you Holy Father in the name of all my brothers,' began Esteban. 'We are very happy with your visit because you bring us peace, justice, the love and light of Christ. We hope that you bring us happiness which will endure. We are a humble people. We suffer a great deal. The cows are better off than we are. We are not able to express our feelings and so we keep our suffering in the secrecy of our hearts. We are without work and there is no-one to help us. Nevertheless, we willingly place our feeble strength at your service. We offer it to your Church and ours. Holy Father, ask the Holy Spirit to help your poor children. The Indians ask you, through me, to pray that the

Word of God may be fulfilled in our lives.'

A tape-recording of these words was given to the Pope so that he should be able to hear them again at leisure. This was an unusual but highly valued gift. When Esteban finished his speech, there was, for a time, an even greater silence than that which had accompanied it and the deep emotion which his words aroused was revealed. But this lasted no more than a few moments. This was, after all, a joyful day in honour of the Holy Father and so it should continue to be. Containing his own emotion with difficulty, the Pope replied to Esteban in the following words:

Beloved Brothers, Indios and Peasants,

I greet you with joy and I am grateful for your enthusiastic presence and the words of welcome you have addressed to me. I cannot find a better greeting to express to you the sentiments that now fill my heart than the sentence of St Peter, first Pope of the Church: 'Peace to all of you that are in Christ.' Peace to you, who form such a large group.

You, too, inhabitants of Oaxaca, Chiapas, Culiacán and those who have come from so many other parts, heirs to the blood and the culture of your noble ancestors – particularly the Mixtecs and the Zapotecs – were 'called to be saints together with all those who call on the name of our Lord Jesus Christ' (1 Cor. 1:2).

The Son of God 'dwelt among us' to make sons of God those who believe in his name (cf. Jn. 1:11ff.); and he entrusted to the Church the continuation of this mission of salvation wherever there are men. So it is not surprising that one day, in the already distant sixteenth century, intrepid missionaries arrived here out of faithfulness to the Church, eager to assimilate your life-style and customs in order to reveal better, and give a living expression to, the image of Christ. Let our grateful memory go to the first Bishop of Oaxaca, Juan José López de Zárate and the many other missionaries – Franciscans, Dominicans, Augustinians, and Jesuits – men whose faith and human generosity are worthy of admiration.

They were well aware how important culture is as a vehicle to transmit the faith, in order that men may progress in knowledge of God. In this there can be no distinction of race or of culture, 'there cannot be Greek and Jew, . . . slave, freeman, but Christ is all, and in all' (cf. Col. 3:9–11). This is a challenge and a stimulus for the Church, since, being faithful to the genuine and complete message of the Lord, she must open up and interpret the whole human reality in order to instil the strength of the Gospel into it (cf. *Evangelii Nuntiandi*, nn. 20.40).

Beloved Brothers, my presence among you wishes to be a living and authentic sign of this universal concern of the Church. The Pope and the Church are with you and love you: they love your persons, your culture, your traditions; they admire your marvellous past, they encourage you in the present and they hope so much for the future.

But it is not just of this that I want to speak to you. Through you, Indios and peasants, there appears before me the immense multitude of the rural world, which is still the prevalent part in the Latin-American continent and a very large sector, even nowadays, in our planet.

Before this imposing spectacle reflected in my eyes, I cannot but think of the identical picture that my predecessor Paul VI contemplated, ten years ago, in his memorable visit to Colombia and, more concretely, in his meeting with the peasants.

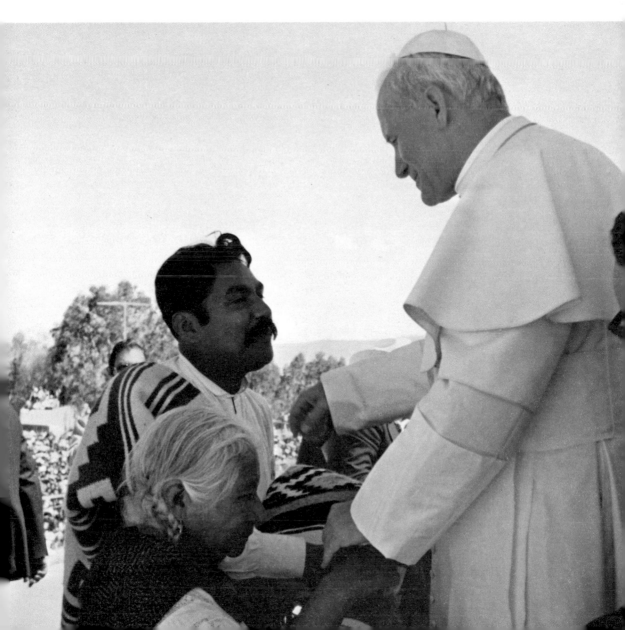

I want to repeat with him — if it were possible in an even stronger tone of voice — that the present Pope wishes 'to be in solidarity with your cause, which is the cause of humble people, of the poor' (Address to Peasants, 23 August 1968). The Pope is with these masses of the population that are 'nearly always abandoned at an ignoble level of life and sometimes harshly treated and exploited' (ibidem).

Adopting the line of my predecessors John XXIII and Paul VI, as well as that of the Second Vatican Council (cf. *Mater et Magistra; Populorum Progressio; Gaudium et Spes*, 9, 71 etc.), and in view of a situation that continues to be alarming, not often better and sometimes even worse, the Pope wishes to be your voice, the voice of those who cannot speak or who are silenced, in order to be the conscience of consciences, an invitation to action, in order to make up for lost time which is often time of prolonged suffering and unsatisfied hopes.

The depressed rural world, the worker who with his sweat waters also his affliction, cannot wait any longer for full and effective recognition of his dignity, which is not inferior to that of any other social sector. He has the right to be respected and not to be deprived, with manoeuvres which are sometimes tantamount to real spoilation, of the little that he has. He has the right to be rid of the barriers of exploitation, often made up of intolerable selfishness, against which his best efforts of advancement are shattered. He has the right to real help — which is not charity or crumbs of justice — in order that he may have access to the development that his dignity as a man and as a son of God deserves.

Therefore it is necessary to act promptly and in depth. It is necessary to carry out bold changes, which are deeply innovatory. It is necessary to undertake urgent reforms without waiting any longer (*Populorum Progressio*, 32).

It cannot be forgotten that the measures to be taken must be adequate. The Church does indeed defend the legitimate right to private property, but she also teaches no less clearly that there is always a social mortgage on all private property, in order that goods may serve the general purpose that God gave them. And if the common good requires it, there should be no hesitation even at expropriation, carried out in the due form *(Populorum Progressio,* 24).

The agricultural world has great importance and great dignity. It is just this world that offers society the products necessary for its nutrition. It is a task that deserves the appreciation and grateful esteem of all, which is a recognition of the dignity of those engaged in it.

A dignity that can and must increase with the contemplation of God, contemplation encouraged by contact with nature, reflection of the divine action which looks after the grass in the fields, makes it grow, nourishes it; which makes the land fertile, sending it rain and wind, so that it may feed also animals, which help man, as we read at the beginning of Genesis.

Work in the fields involves great difficulties because of the effort it demands, the contempt with which it is sometimes considered and the obstacles it meets with; difficulties which only a far-reaching action can solve. Otherwise, the flight from the countryside to the cities will continue, frequently creating problems of extensive and distressing proletarization, overcrowding in houses unworthy of human peoples, and so on.

An evil that is quite widespread is the tendency to individualism among rural workers, whereas a better co-ordinated and united action could be of great help. Think of this too, dear sons.

In spite of all this, the rural world possesses enviable human and religious riches: a deep-rooted love of the family; the sense of friendship; help for the needy; deep humanism; love of peace and civil society; a deep religious sense; trust and opening to God; promotion of love for the Blessed Virgin; and so many others. It is a well-deserved tribute of recognition that the Pope wishes to express to you, and for which society is indebted to you. Thank you, rural workers, for your precious contribution to social good; mankind owes you a great deal.

On your side, leaders of the peoples, powerful classes which sometimes keep unproductive lands that hide the bread that so many families lack, human conscience, the conscience of peoples, the cry of the destitute, and above all the voice of God, the voice of the Church, repeat to you with me: It is not just, it is not human, it is not Christian to continue with certain situations that are clearly unjust. It is necessary to carry out real, effective measures – at the local, national, and international level – along the broad line marked by the encyclical *Mater et Magistra* (part three). It is clear that those who must collaborate most in this, are those who can do most.

Beloved Brothers and Sons, work at your human elevation, but do not stop here. Make yourselves more and more worthy in the moral and religious field. Do not harbour feelings of hatred and violence, but look towards the Master and Lord of all, who gives each one the reward that his acts deserve. The Church is with you and encourages you to live your condition as sons of God, united with Christ, under the gaze of Mary, our Holy Mother.

The Pope asks you for your prayer and offers you his. And blessing all of you and your families, he takes leave of you with the words of the Apostle St Paul: 'Greet all the brethren with a holy kiss.' Let this be a call to hope. Amen.

The Pope's speech was loudly
applauded. After watching a spectacle of
local dancing — excerpts from the *fiesta
de la guelaguetza* — the Pope took his
leave of a delegation of Indians, who
represented the remainder of their
people, and he showed special affection
for a number of children who were
brought to him. One of these put on his
head one of the typical hats, worn by the
dancing troupe a short while before.

THE CONFERMENT OF MINOR ORDERS

The Pope's helicopter returned to the airport of Oaxaca about 1 p.m. The Pope was carried into the city in an open car protected from the sun by a large umbrella and cheered by an enthusiastic crowd along the thirteen kilometres of the route. Behind the double line of people were their *adobes,* miserable dwellings of straw and mud, a melancholy witness to their sorry plight.

As he drove along, the Pope passed under many arches adorned with white and yellow carnations. A number of slogans had been composed in multi-coloured flowers, such as 'Welcome John Paul II. Man of peace and of respect for human life' and many others. The most striking perhaps was above an archway close to the city. It said 'You are the voice of the silent'.

Once again, inside the town, popular enthusiasm was displayed by dancing and music, explosions of fireworks and petards, the scattering of balloons, confetti and flower petals.

The Pope made a brief halt at the Minor Seminary of Oaxaca. At 4 p.m., still in an open car, he drove to the Cathedral to celebrate Mass in the Cathedral square before a large and reverent crowd of about 250,000 people. In the course of the ceremony, he conferred upon ten Indians the minor orders of lectors and acolytes. The principal moments of the rite were accompanied by the music of a band of Mitjes Indians who had come along especially from a neighbouring village.

Beloved Brothers and Sisters,

This ceremony, in which, with immense joy, I confer some sacred ministries on descendants of the ancient races of this land of America, confirms the truth of a saying of a high personality of your country to my venerated predecessor Paul VI: from the beginning of the history of the American nations it was above all the Church that protected the most humble, their dignity and value as human persons.

Today the truth of this affirmation receives a new confirmation, now that the Bishop of Rome and Pastor of the universal Church will call some of them to collaborate with his pastors in service of the ecclesial community, for its greater growth and vitality (cf. *Evangelii Nuntiandi* n. 73).

1. It is well known that these ministries do not change laymen into ecclesiastics: those who receive them continue to be laymen, that is, they do not leave the state in which they were living when they were called (cf. 1 Cor. 7:20). And even when they co-operate, as substitutes or helpers, with consecrated ministers, these laymen are, above all, collaborators of God (cf. 1 Cor. 3:9), who avails himself also of them to carry out his will to save all men (cf. 1 Tim. 2:4).

What is more, precisely because these laymen commit themselves deliberately to this plan of salvation, to such an extent that this commitment is for them the ultimate reason of their presence in the world (cf. St John Chrysostom, *In Act. Ap.* 20:4), they must be considered as archetypes of the participation of all the faithful in the Church's mission of salvation.

2. Actually, all the faithful, by virtue of their baptism and of the sacrament of confirmation, must profess publicly the faith received from God by means of the Church, spread it and defend it as true witnesses of Christ (cf. *Lumen Gentium* n. 11). That is, they are called to evangelization, which is a fundamental duty of all the members of the people of God (cf. *Ad Gentes,* n. 35), whether or not they have special functions more closely connected with the duties of Pastors (*Apostolicam Actuositatem* n. 24).

In this connection let the successor of Peter make a fervent appeal to one and all to assimilate and practise the teachings and directions of the Second Vatican Council, which dedicated to the laity chapter four of the dogmatic constitution *Lumen Gentium,* and the decree *Apostolicam Actuositatem.*

I also wish, as a memory of my passing in your midst, though also with my eyes fixed on the faithful of the whole world, to refer briefly to what is peculiar to the co-operation of the laity in the one apostolate of the Church, its expressions, both individual and associated, its determinant characteristic. To do so, I will take inspiration from the invocation to Christ which we read in the prayer of Lauds of this Monday of the fourth week of ordinary liturgical time: 'You who operate with the Father in the history of humanity, renew men and things with the force of your Spirit.'

In fact, the laity, who by divine vocation participate in the entire reality of the world, instilling into it their faith, which has become a reality in their own public and private life (cf. James 2:17), are the most immediate protagonists of the renewal of men and of things. With their active presence as believers, they work at the progressive consecration of the world to God (cf. *Lumen Gentium* n. 34). This presence is linked with the whole economy of the Christian religion, which is, indeed, a doctrine, but is above all an event: the event of the Incarnation, Jesus, the God-man who recapitulated in himself the universe (cf. Eph. 1:10). It corresponds to the example of Christ, who made physical contact, too, a vehicle of communication of his restoring power (cf. Mk. 1:41 and 7:33; Mt. 9:29ff. and 20:34; Lk. 7:14 and 8:54). It is inherent in the sacramental nature of the Church, which, having been made a sign and instrument of the union of men with God and of the unity of the whole of mankind (cf. *Lumen Gentium* n. 1), has been called by God to be in permanent communion with the world in order to be in it the leaven that transforms it from within (cf. Mt. 13:33).

The apostolate of the laity, understood and put into practice, in this way, gives to all the events of human history their full meaning, respecting their autonomy and encouraging the progress required by the very nature of each of them. At the same time, it gives us the key to interpret fully the meaning of history, since all temporal realities, like the events that manifest them, take on their deepest meaning in the spiritual dimension that establishes the relationship between the present and the future (cf. Heb. 13:14). Disregard or mutilation of this dimension would become, in fact, an attack on the very essence of man.

3. On leaving this land, I take with me a pleasant memory of you, that of having met generous souls who, from now, will offer their lives for the spreading of the kingdom of God. At the same time I am sure that, like trees planted near rivers, they will yield abundant fruit in due course (cf. Ps. 1:3) for the consolidation of the Gospel.

Take heart! Be the leaven in the dough (Mt. 13:33), form the Church! May your witness arouse everywhere other heralds of salvation: 'How beautiful are the feet of those who preach good news!' (Rom. 10:15). Let us thank God who 'began a good work in you (and) will bring it to completion at the day of Jesus Christ' (Phil. 1:6).

TALK TO REPRESENTATIVES
OF CATHOLIC ORGANIZATIONS

The Pope flew back to Mexico City on the
Boeing 727 and returned to the Apostolic
Delegation at about 7.30 p.m. There he
received in audience representatives of
the Catholic National Organizations to
whom he addressed the following
speech:

Beloved Sons of the national Catholic Organizations of Mexico,

Blessed be the Lord who permits me also — in my stay in this beloved land
of Our Lady of Guadalupe — to have the joy of a meeting with you.

I am grateful to you for your lively demonstrations of filial affection,
and I can confess to you how much I would like to stop with each of you
to get to know you personally, to know more about your ecclesial service,
and to dwell on so many fundamental aspects of your apostolic project. In
any case, I wish, these words to be an eloquent testimony of closeness,
appreciation, stimulus and guidance of your best efforts as laity — and as
organized Catholic laity — on the part of him who, as the successor of
Peter, has been called to the service of all servants of the Lord.

You know very well how the Second Vatican Council took up this great
contemporary historical movement of the 'advancement of the laity',
studying it in its theological foundations, integrating it and illuminating it
completely in the ecclesiology of *Lumen Gentium,* convoking and giving
impetus to the active participation of laity in the life and mission of the
Church. In the Body of Christ constituted in 'plurality of ministries but
unity of mission' (*A.A.* n. 2, cf. *L.G.* 10, 32. . .), laity as Christian
faithful 'are by baptism made one body with Christ and are established
among the People of God. They are in their own way made sharers in the
priestly, prophetic, and kingly functions of Christ'. They are called to
exercise their apostolate, in particular 'in each and in all of the secular
professions and occupations' which they carry out, and 'in the ordinary
circumstances of family and social life' (*L.G.* 31), in order to 'penetrate and
perfect the temporal sphere with the spirit of the gospel' (*A.A.* N. 5).

In the overall framework of the conciliar teachings and especially in the
light of the 'Constitution on the Church', vast requirements and renewed
prospects of lay action were opened in very varied fields of ecclesial and
secular life. Without disparaging the individual apostolate, which is
recognized as its inescapable premise, the decree *Apostolicam Actuositatem*
also pointed out the Church's appreciation of the associative forms of the
lay apostolate, congenial to the Church's community nature and to the
evangelization requirements of the modern world.

You are, then, signs and protagonists of this 'advancement of the laity'
which has yielded so much fruit for ecclesial life in these years of the
implementation of the Council. I call upon you and, through you, upon all

laity and lay associations of the Latin American Church to renew a double dimension of your lay and ecclesial commitment. On the one hand, to bear witness to Christ effectively, to confess with joy and docility your full faithfulness to the ecclesial magisterium, to ensure your filial obedience and collaboration with your Pastors, to seek the most adequate organic and dynamic integration of your apostolate in the mission of the Church and, in particular, in the apostolate of your local Churches. The Mexican laity has given and gives many and tested examples of this. And it is with joy and gratitude that I wish to recall in particular the commemoration, in this year, 1979, of the fiftieth anniversary of Mexican Catholic Action; the backbone of the organized laity in the country.

The Third General Conference of the Latin American Episcopate is a vital moment of grace which demands personal and community conversion in order to renew your ecclesial communion, your trust in your Pastors, your vigour and renewed apostolic effort.

On the other hand, from this ecclesial perspective, I wish to call you to renew your human and Christian awareness of the other side of your commitment: participation in the necessities, aspirations, and crucial challenges with which the reality of your neighbour calls for your evangelizing action as Christian laity.

Among the vast expanse of the fields that call for the presence of the laity in the world, and which are pointed out by the apostolic Exhortation *Evangelii Nuntiandi* — this magna charta of evangelization — I wish to mention some fundamental and urgent spaces in the accelerated and unequal process of industrialization, urbanization, and cultural transformation in the lives of your peoples.

The safeguarding, advancement, sanctification, and apostolic projection of family life must count Catholic laity among their most decisive and consistent agents. The basic cell of the social tissue, which was considered by the Second Vatican Council as the 'domestic Church', requires an evangelizing effort in order to expand its factors of human and Christian growth and overcome the obstacles that seek to harm its integrity and finality.

The emergent and complex 'worlds' of intellectuals and university students, of the proletariat, technicians and executives, of the vast agricultural sectors and suburban populations subjected to the accelerated impact of economico-social and cultural changes, call for special apostolic attention, sometimes almost missionary, on the part of the Catholic laity in the pastoral projection of the Church as a whole.

How could we fail to mention also the presence, within this challenging multitude, of youth with its restless hopes, rebellions, and frustrations, its unlimited desires, sometimes utopian, its religious sensitivity and quests, as well as its temptations from consumer or ideological idols! The young expect clear, consistent, and joyful testimonies of ecclesial faith which will help them to restructure and canalize their own open and generous energies in solid options of personal and collective life. Let charity, the vital sap of ecclesial life, be manifested also by means of

Christian laity in brotherly solidarity before the situations of indigence, oppression, helplessness or solitude of the poorest, the favourites of the liberating and redeeming Lord.

How could we forget the whole world of teaching, where the men of tomorrow are forged; even the field of politics, in order that it may always respond to criteria of the common good; the field of international organizations, in order that they may be schools of justice, hope and understanding among peoples; the world of medicine and of the health service where so many interventions are possible which very closely concern the moral order; the field of culture and art, fertile grounds to contribute to making man worthy on the human and on the spiritual plane?

In this twofold effort of renewed Christian commitment, your ecclesial faithfulness, gathering and strengthening the tradition of the Mexican laity, will set you going again with new energies to operate as a ferment, creating wider perspectives of social life.

The task is an immense one. You are called to take part in it, assuming and continuing the best of the experience of ecclesial and secular participation in recent years; gradually leaving aside crises of identity, sterile contestations, and ideologies extraneous to the Gospel.

One of the phenomena of recent years which has manifested with ever increasing vigour the dynamism of the laity in Latin America and elsewhere has been that of the so-called grass-roots communities (*communautés de base*), which have arisen coincidently with the crisis of the movement towards groupings among Catholics.

The grass-roots communities can be a valid instrument of formation and of religious life within a new environment of Christian impulse, and they can be useful, among other things, for a widespread penetration of the Gospel in society.

But that this may be possible it is necessary that they bear well in mind the criteria so clearly expressed by the Apostolic Exhortation *Evangelii Nuntiandi* (n. 58), so that they may be nourished by the word of God in prayer, and remain united, not separated, and still less in opposition to the Church, to the Pastors and to other ecclesial groups or associations.

As up to today, and increasingly better, may your associations form Christians with a vocation of holiness, staunch in their faith, certain in the doctrine proposed by the authentic Magisterium, firm and active in the Church, united in a deep spiritual life, nourished by frequent reception of the sacraments of Penance and of the Eucharist, persevering in testimony and evangelical action, consistent and effective in their temporal commitments, constant promoters of peace and justice against all violence and oppression, acute in critical discernment of situations and ideologies in the light of the social teachings of the Church, trusting in the hope of the Lord.

Let my Apostolic Blessing go to you, to all the laity of your associations, to your ecclesiastical assistants, and to the Mexican laity as a whole; and also to the millions of Latin American laity who are raising their prayer and putting their hopes in Puebla. I entrust you all to the motherly protection of the Blessed Mary, in her title of Guadalupe.

I Come to You
as a Brother

Tuesday 30 January

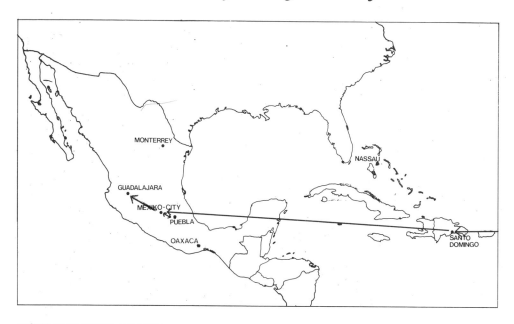

WITH THE BOYS OF THE MIGUEL ANGEL SCHOOL

The Pope's love of youngsters has earned him the title of the Children's Pope. It was very noticeable in Mexico. Children and students regarded him as 'their' Pope. During his Mexican pilgrimage, John Paul II repeated the affectionate gestures of sympathy towards children so often seen during his audiences or pastoral visits in Rome. He began the day with a visit to the Catholic school called the Miguel Angel Institute before proceeding to the famous basilica and shrine of Our Lady of Zapopan. The children waited for him expectantly for hours, sacrificing their night's sleep. When he appeared, there was a frantic outburst of applause. John Paul II responded with wide gestures of the arms, quite overcome by such a demonstration of enthusiasm. His meeting with the students enabled him to talk to them about education and the function of religious instruction:

Dear Young People,

I am happy to be able to meet you today in this Catholic school, the 'Miguel Angel' institute. You form a large group of all ages, both you who study in this institute and you who come from other Catholic schools. I see and feel to be present in your youth all the students of the country. I greet you all with special affection, because I see in you the promising hope of the Church and of the Mexican nation of the future.

I also wish to greet affectionately your teachers, the representatives of the institutes of formation and of fathers of a family. You all deserve my respect because you are all engaged in forming the new generations.

1. The difficulties that Catholic schools in Mexico have been able to overcome in carrying out their mission is another reason for my gratitude to the Lord and, at the same time it is a stimulus for your responsibility, in order that the Catholic schools may complete the integral formation of future citizens on a really human and Christian basis.

'The Church, as regards her specific mission, must promote and impart Christian education, to which all the baptized are entitled so that they may reach the maturity of faith. As the servant of all men, the Church tries to collaborate through her members, especially laity, in tasks of human cultural advancement, in all forms that interest society.' (Medellín. Education, n. 9.)

2. The Church contemplates youth with optimism and deep hope. You, the young, represent the majority of the Mexican population, fifty per cent of which are under twenty years of age. In the most difficult moments of Christianity in Mexican history, the young have borne witness heroically and generously.

The Church sees in youth an enormous innovatory force, which our predecessor John XXIII considered a symbol of the Church herself, called to a constant renewal of herself, that is, to an incessant rejuvenation.

Prepare for life with seriousness and diligence. At this moment of youth, so important for the full maturing of your personality, always give an adequate place to the religious element in your formation, the one that brings man to attainment of his full dignity, which is that of being a son of God. Always remember that only if one builds, as St Paul says, on the one foundation which is Jesus Christ (cf. 1 Cor. 3:11), will one be able to construct something really great and lasting.

3. As a memory of this meeting, so cordial and joyful, I wish to leave you a concrete consideration.

With the vivacity that is characteristic of your age, with the generous enthusiasm of your young hearts, walk towards Christ. He alone is the solution to all your problems. He alone is the way, the truth, and the life; he alone is the real salvation of the world; he alone is the hope of mankind.

Seek Jesus; endeavouring to acquire a deep personal faith that will inform and direct your whole life. But, above all, let it be your commitment and your programme to love Jesus, with a sincere, authentic, and personal love. He must be your friend and your support along the path of life. He alone has words of eternal life (cf. Jn. 6:68).

Your thirst for the absolute cannot be quenched with ideological substitutes that lead to hatred, violence, and despair. Christ alone, sought and loved with sincere love, is a source of joy, serenity, and peace.

But after having met Christ, after having discovered who he is, you cannot fail to feel the necessity of proclaiming him. Be real witnesses of Christ; live and proclaim your faith with deeds and with words.

You, beloved young people, must have the concern and the desire to be bearers of Christ to this modern society, which needs him more than ever, which is more than ever in search of him, in spite of the fact that appearances sometimes induce us to believe the contrary.

'Young people who are well trained in faith and prayer', wrote my predecessor Paul VI in the exhortation *Evangelii Nuntiandi,* 'must become more and more the apostles of youth.' (n. 72.) Each of you has the stirring task of being a proclaimer of Christ among your schoolmates and playmates. Each of you must have in your heart the desire to be an apostle among those around you.

4. I now wish to confide in you a problem that is very near my heart. The Church is aware of the under-development that exists in many areas of the Latin American continent and your country. My predecessor Paul VI, in his encyclical *Populorum Progressio* affirmed: '. . . basic education is the primary object of any plan of development' (n. 35).

In the accelerated dynamics of change, characteristic of modern society, it is necessary and sometimes urgent for us to be able to create an atmosphere of human and Christian solidarity round the difficult problem of schooling. The Council already recalled this in its Document on Education: 'All men of whatever race, condition or age, in virtue of their dignity as human persons, have an inalienable right to education.' (n. 1.)

It is not possible to remain indifferent before the serious problem of illiteracy or semi-illiteracy.

At one of the decisive moments for the future of Latin America, I make strong appeal in Christ's name to all men and, particularly, to you young people, to give, today and tomorrow, your help, service, and collaboration, in this task of schooling. My voice, my fatherly supplication, goes also to Christian educators in order that, with their contribution, they may promote literacy campaigns and 'culturalization' with a complete view of man. Let us not forget that 'an illiterate is a person with an undernourished mind' (*P.P.* 35).

I trust in the collaboration of all to help to solve this problem which regards such an essential right of the human being.

Young people! Commit yourselves as men and Christians to things that deserve effort, disinterestedness, and generosity. The Church expects it from you and trusts you!

5. Let us place this intention at the feet of Mary, whom Mexicans invoke as Our Lady of Guadalupe. She was closely associated with the mystery of Christ and is an example of generous love and dedication to the service of others. Her life of deep faith is the way to strengthen our faith and it teaches us to meet God in the deep recesses of our being.

Youth Associations and groups of friends, on returning home, tell everyone that the Pope counts on the young. Say that the young are the strength and the consolation of the Pope, who wishes to be with them so that they may hear his voice of encouragement amid all the difficulties that integration in society involves.

May the apostolic blessing which I willingly impart to you, to your dear ones, and to all those dedicated to your formation, help you and stimulate you to carry out your resolutions.

AT GUADALAJARA

Guadalajara is one of the principal cities of Mexico, a great industrial and sporting centre. John Paul II travelled there by air, in a plane supplied by the President of the Republic. The flight took about one hour. At the airport, he was received by the Archbishop of Guadalajara, Cardinal José Salazar, who welcomed him on behalf of the local church which is distinguished by the fervour of its good works, its institutions and its apostolate. After listening to the Cardinal's speech of welcome, the Pope replied:

Lord Cardinal, Beloved Brothers and Sons,

I warmly thank the Archbishop of Guadalajara for the greeting he kindly addressed to me at the moment of my arrival in this beloved archdiocese. The Pope feels moved by the welcome, so human, so Christian and so familiar. I feel as if I were among my own people, at home.

In the history of this great country, you the inhabitants of this state and this city have always distinguished yourselves by your spirit of religion and of work. You have known how to unite the spiritual and the material in a synthesis that is based on real experience of the message of the Son of God.

My beloved friends: my greeting goes to those present here, and particularly to the priests, religious, and all those who work in the construction of the kingdom of God in this archdiocese, rich in testimony of Christian faith which is manifested in so many ways, especially in vocations to religious life.

Thank you for the opportunity which you offer your Father to be with you, my sons, on this visit.

May the Lord bless you!

AT THE SANTA CECILIA QUARTER

The Pope was flown by helicopter to the centre of Guadalajara which, even today, retains its Spanish appearance. The first stop was in the quarter of Santa Cecilia. The name evokes those musical corporations which are a feature of Guadalajara, but also an area of great poverty where life is a daily drama. Workers and unemployed yearn for a just reward and more decent living standards. The Pope assured them of the Church's backing:

Beloved Brothers and Sisters,

I keenly desired this meeting, inhabitants of the district of Santa Cecilia, because I feel solidarity with you and because, being poor, you are entitled to my particular concern.

I tell you the reason at once: the Pope loves you because you are God's favourites. He himself, on founding his family, the Church, kept poor and needy humanity in mind. To redeem it, he sent precisely his Son, who was born poor and lived among the poor in order to make us rich with his poverty (cf. 2 Cor. 8:9).

As a consequence of this redemption, carried out in him who became one of us, we are now no longer poor servants, we are sons, who can call God 'Father' (cf. Gal. 4:4–6). We are no longer abandoned, since, if we are sons of God, we are also heirs to the goods he offers abundantly to those who love him (Mt. 11:28). Could we doubt that a father gives good things to his children? (cf. Mt. 7:7ff.). Jesus himself, our Saviour, waits for us in order to relieve us when we are weary (cf. Mt. 11:28). At the same time, he counts on our personal collaboration to make us more and more worthy, being the architects of our own human and moral elevation.

At the same time, faced with your overwhelming situation, I call with all my strength on those who have means and who feel they are Christians, to renew their minds and their hearts in order that, promoting greater justice and even giving something of their own, no one will lack proper food, clothing, housing, culture and work; all that gives dignity to the human person. The image of Christ on the Cross, the price of the redemption of humanity, is a pressing appeal to spend our lives in putting ourselves in the service of the needy, in harmony with charity, which is generous and which does not sympathize with injustice, but with truth (cf. 1 Cor. 13:2ff.).

I bless you all, asking the Lord always to illuminate your hearts and your actions.

113

IN THE FOOTBALL STADIUM

The Pope continued his visit in the helicopter, flying to the Jalisco Stadium, where a hundred thousand workers were waiting to greet him. Among the gifts offered to him there was one of a peculiarly sporting character — an image of Christ the Footballer. This was certainly an unusual holy picture but one which expressed the feelings of those young men whose zeal for athletics is combined with the ideals of faith. The crowd acclaimed the Holy Father with shouts of 'Long live the sporting Pope'. John Paul II had a message for these workers also, in which he emphasized the nobility of work and the rights and duties pertaining to it as well as its social and supernatural aims:

Dear Brothers and Sisters,

Dear Workers,

I arrive here in the magnificent setting of Guadalajara, where we meet in the name of him who wished to be known as the carpenter's son.

I come to you, having before my eyes and in my soul the image of Our Lady of Guadalupe, your patron saint, for whom you profess a filial love that I have been able to see not only in her sanctuary but also passing through the streets and cities of Mexico. Where there is a Mexican, there is the Mother of Guadalupe. A gentleman told me that ninety-six per cent of Mexicans are Catholics, but one hundred per cent are Guadalupans.

I wished to come and visit you, working-class families of Guadalajara and of other localities in this archdiocese, which is distinguished by its adherence to the faith, its family unity and its efforts to meet, in God's name, the great human and Christian requirements of justice, peace, and progress.

I present myself to you as a brother, joyfully and lovingly, after having had the opportunity to travel through the streets of Mexico and to witness the love that is professed here for Christ, for the Blessed Virgin, and for the Pope — a pilgrim and messenger of faith, hope, and union among men.

I wish to express to you, right away, how happy the Pope is that this is a meeting with workers, with working-class families, with Christian families which, from their places of work, know how to be agents of social welfare, respect, love of God, in the workshop, in the factory, in any house or place.

I think of you, boys and girls, young people of working-class families; there comes into my mind the figure of him who was born in an artisan's family, who grew in age, wisdom, and grace, who learned from his Mother human ways, and who had his teacher in life and in daily work in the just man that God gave him as father. The Church venerates this Mother and this man; this holy worker, model of a man and, at the same time, of a worker.

Our Lord Jesus Christ received the caresses of his strong worker's hands, hands hardened by work, but open to kindness and to needy brothers. Allow me to enter your homes; yes, you want to have the Pope as your guest and friend, and to give him the consolation of seeing in your homes the union and the family love which gives rest, after a hard day's work, in this relationship of mutual affection that reigned in the Holy Family. It shows me, dear children and young people, that you are preparing seriously for the future; I repeat to you, you are the hope of the Pope.

Do not deny me the joy of seeing you walk along paths that lead you to be real followers of good, and friends of Christ. Do not deny me the joy of your sense of responsibility in studies, activities, and amusements. You are called to be bearers of generosity and honesty, to fight against immorality, to prepare a more just, healthier, and happier Mexico for the sons of God and sons of our mother Mary.

You know very well that the work of your parents is present in the common effort of growth of this nation and in everything that contributes to bring the benefits of modern civilization to all Mexicans. Be proud of your parents, and collaborate with them in your formation as honoured and Christian young people; my affection and my encouragement accompany you.

The Pope's affection also goes to the working mothers and brides present, and to all those listening to my words by means of the media of social communication. Remember that Virgin Mary who knew how to be a cause of joy for her husband and a solicitous guide for her son in moments of difficulty and hardship. When there are worries and limitations, remember that God chose a poor mother and that she succeeded in remaining firm in good, even in the hardest hours.

Many of you also work in one of the multiple activities that are opening to women's capacities today; many of you are also bread-winners for a good many homes, and a continual help in order that family life may be more and more dignified. Be present with your creativity in the transformation of this society. The modern way of life offers more and more important opportunities and posts for women; enlightened by your religious sense, make your contribution to all your fellow citizens, and even to the highest authorities.

Friends, worker brothers, there is a Christian conception of work, of family and social life. It contains great values, and demands moral criteria and norms in order to direct those who believe in God and in Jesus Christ; in order that work may be carried out as a real vocation to change the world, in a spirit of service and of love for brothers; in order that the human person may reach fulfilment here and contribute to the growing humanization of the world and its structures.

Work is not a curse, it is a blessing from God who calls man to rule the earth and transform it, in order that the divine work of creation may continue with man's intelligence and effort. I want to tell you with all my soul and with all my might that I suffer at the lack of work, I suffer at the ideologies of hate and of violence that are not evangelical and that cause so many wounds in mankind today.

It is not enough for the Christian to denounce injustices, he is asked to be a real witness and promoter of justice; he who works has rights that he

must defend legally, but he also has duties which he must carry out generously. As Christians you are called to be architects of justice and of real freedom as well as forgers of social charity. Modern technique creates a whole set of new problems and sometimes produces unemployment. But it also opens great possibilities that ask of the worker increasing qualifications, as also the contribution of his human capacities and his creative imagination. For this reason, work must not be a mere necessity, but it must be considered a real vocation, a call from God to build a new world in which justice and brotherhood dwell, a foretaste of the Kingdom of God, in which there will certainly not be shortages or limitations.

Work must be the means in order that the whole of creation will be subjected to the dignity of the human being and son of God. Work offers the opportunity to commit oneself with the whole community without resentment, without bitterness, without hatred, but with the universal love of Christ that excludes no one and embraces everyone.

Christ proclaimed to us the Gospel from which we know that God is love, that he is the Father of all, and that we are all brothers.

The central mystery of our Christian life, the paschal mystery, makes us look to the New Heaven and to the New Earth. This paschal mystery must exist in work. Through it, sacrifices and efforts are accepted with Christian impetus in order to bring about that the new order willed by the Lord may shine forth more clearly, and to construct a world that will correspond to God's goodness in harmony, peace and love.

Beloved Sons and Daughters, I pray to the Lord for all of you and your families. I pray to the Lord for the unity and stability of your marriages, and that your home life will always be full and joyful. Christian faith must be stronger in the presence of all the factors of the modern crisis. The Church, as the Council taught us affectionately, must be a large family in which lives the dynamic of unity, life, joy, and love, which is the Holy Trinity.

The same Council called the family a 'little Church'; in the Christian family the evangelizing action of the Church begins. Families are the first schools of education to the faith, and only if this Christian unity is preserved will it be possible for the Church to carry out her mission in society and in the Church herself.

Friends and Brothers, thank you for having offered me the possibility of taking part in this great meeting with the world of workers, with whom I always feel so much at ease. You are friends and companions for the Pope. Thank you.

This city of Guadalajara has distinguished itself in the whole of Mexico for the impetus given to sports activities which bestow on the family physical and spiritual development, and the joy of a healthy mind in a healthy body. The group of footballers that accompanies us gives our great meeting a new colour. The Pope gives his blessing to one and all of you. May it encourage you in your apostilic commitment with generous brotherly dedication, and with the certainty that God is working with you in order that you may construct a world that is more beautiful, kind, just, human and Christian. Amen.

WITH THE NUNS IN CLAUSURA

In the Cathedral, the Pope talked to the nuns in the enclosed orders. To these he recalled the value of the contemplative life as a witness to the promise of the Kingdom and as an expression of the union with others who are absorbed with the cares of family life and of worldly affairs:

Beloved Enclosed Sisters,

In this Cathedral of Guadalajara, I wish to greet you with the beautiful and expressive words that we frequently repeat in the liturgical assembly: 'May the Lord be with you.' (Roman Missal.) Yes, may the Lord, to whom you have dedicated your whole life, always be with you.

How could a meeting of the Pope with contemplative Sisters fail to take place during the visit to Mexico? If I would like to see so many persons, you have a special place because of your particular consecration to the Lord and to the Church. For this reason, the Pope, too, wishes to be close to you.

This meeting wishes to be the continuation of the one I had with other Mexican Sisters. I said many things to them which are also for you, but now I wish to refer to what is more specifically yours.

How often the Magisterium of the Church has shown its great esteem for, and appreciation of, your life dedicated to prayer, silence and to an exceptional way of dedication to God! In these moments when everything is changing so much, does this type of life continue to have a meaning or is it something that is already outdated?

The Pope tells you: Yes, your life is more important than ever, your complete consecration is fully relevant today. In a world that is losing the sense of the divine, in the light of the over-estimation of material things, you, beloved Sisters, committed from your cloisters to be witnesses of certain values for which you live, be witnesses to the Lord for the world of today, and instil with your prayer a new breath of life into the Church and into modern man.

Especially in contemplative life, it is a question of realizing a difficult unity: to manifest to the world the mystery of the Church in this world and to enjoy here already, teaching them to men, as St Paul says, 'the things that are above' (Col. 3:1).

Being a contemplative does not mean breaking radically with the world, with the apostolate. The contemplative has to find her specific way of extending the kingdom of God, of collaborating in the building up of the earthly city, not only with her prayers and sacrifices, but also with her testimony, silent, it is true, yet which can be understood by the men of good will with whom she is in contact.

For this reason you have to find your own style which, within a

contemplative vision, will let you share with your brothers the gratuitous gift of God.

Your consecrated life comes from baptismal consecration and expresses it with greater fullness. With a free response to the call of the Holy Spirit, you decided to follow Christ, consecrating yourselves to him completely. 'The more stable and firm this bond (the unbreakable bond of union that exists between Christ and his Church) is,' – the Council says – 'the more perfect will the Christian's religious consecration be.' *(Lumen Gentium,* 4.)

You contemplative religious women feel an attraction that brings you to the Lord. Relying on God, you abandon yourselves to his fatherly action which raises you to him and transforms you for eternal contemplation which is the ultimate goal for us all. How could you advance along this path and be faithful to the grace that animates you, if you did not respond with your whole being, by means of a dynamism the impulse of which is love, to this call that directs you permanently to God? So, consider any other activity as a testimony, offered to the Lord, of your deep communion with him, so that he may grant you that purity of intention which is so necessary in order to meet him in prayer itself. In this way you will contribute to the extension of the kingdom of God, with the testimony of your life and with a 'hidden apostolic fruitfulness' *(Perfectae Caritatis,* 7).

Gathered in Christ's name, your communities have as their centre the Eucharist, 'a sacrament of love, a sign of unity, a bond of charity' *(Sacrosanctum Concilium,* 47).

Through the Eucharist, the world also is present at the centre of your life of prayer and offering, as the Council explained: 'Let no one think that their consecrated way of life alienates religious from other men or makes them useless for human society. Though in some cases they have no direct relations with their contemporaries, still in a deeper way they have their fellow men present with them in the heart of Christ and co-operate with them spiritually, so that the building up of human society may always have its foundation in the Lord and have him as its goal: otherwise those who build it may have laboured in vain.' *(Lumen Gentium,* 46.)

Contemplating you with the tenderness of the Lord when he called his disciples 'little flock' (cf. Lk. 12:32) and announced to them that his Father had been pleased to give them the Kingdom, I beg you: keep the simplicity of the 'little ones' of the Gospel. Know how to find it in intimate and deep relations with Christ and in contact with your brothers. You will then know 'overflowing joy through the action of the Holy Spirit', the joy of those who are introduced into the secrets of the Kingdom (cf. *Apostolic Exhortation on the Renewal of Religious Life,* 54).

May the beloved Mother of the Lord, whom you invoke in Mexico with the sweet name of Our Lady of Guadalupe, and following whose example you have dedicated your life to God, obtain for you, on your daily path, that unfailing joy that only Jesus can give.

Receive my warm Apostolic Blessing as a great greeting of peace which is not exhausted in you present here, but which extends invisibly to all your contemplative Sisters in Mexico.

Meanwhile, a vast concourse had gathered in the square outside, the Plaza de la Liberación. The Pope went out onto the balcony of the Archbishop's residence and recited the Angelus with the crowd below as he is accustomed to do every Sunday at St Peter's. He concluded by imparting the Apostolic Blessing.

AT THE BASILICA
OF OUR LADY OF ZAPOPAN

The basilica of Our Lady of Zapopan is the centre of the Marian cult in this region. The Franciscans are its custodians and promoters. It is thanks to them that the devotion to the Madonna has become so popular among the faithful. This is a tradition inherited from Saint Francis himself. Christ should not be dissociated from His mother. As there was not enough room for the crowd inside, the Pope said Mass at the entrance to the church. After the Gospel, he preached a sermon:

Beloved Brothers and Sisters,

1. Here we are gathered today in this beautiful sanctuary of Our Lady of the Immaculate Conception of Zapopán, in the great archdiocese of Guadalajara. I did not want to, nor could I, omit this meeting, around the altar of Jesus and at the feet of Most Holy Mary, with the People of God on pilgrimage to this place. This sanctuary of Zapopán is, in fact, another proof, a tangible and consoling one, of the intense devotion that the Mexican people, and with it the whole Latin American people, has professed to Mary Immaculate for centuries.

Like the Guadalupe sanctuary, this one, too, comes from the colonial age. Like the former, its origins go back to the precious evangelization effort of missionaries (in this case, the sons of St Francis) among the 'Indios', so well disposed to receive the message of salvation in Christ and to venerate his holy Mother, conceived without the stain of sin. Thus these peoples perceive the unique and exceptional place of Mary in the fulfilment of God's plan (cf. *Lumen Gentium* n. 53f.), her eminent holiness, and her motherly relationship with us (ibid. 61, 66). From that moment onwards, she, Mary Immaculate, represented in this simple little image, is incorporated in the popular piety of the people of the Archdiocese of Guadalajara, in that of the Mexican nation and of the whole of Latin America. As Mary herself says prophetically in the canticle of the Magnificat, 'All generations will call me blessed' (Lk. 1:48).

2. If this is true of the whole of the Catholic world, how much more it is in Mexico and in Latin America! It can be said that faith and devotion to Mary and to her mysteries belong to the very identity of these peoples, and characterize their popular piety, of which my predecessor Paul VI spoke in the apostolic Exhortation *Evangelii Nuntiandi* (n. 48). This popular piety is not necessarily a vague sentiment, lacking a solid doctrinal basis, a kind of inferior form of religious manifestation. How often it is, on the contrary,

the true expression of the soul of a people, since it is touched by grace and forged by the happy meeting between the work of evangelization and that of local culture, of which the aforesaid Exhortation also spoke (n. 20)! Thus guided and sustained and, if necessary, purified, by the constant action of pastors, and exercised every day in the life of the people, popular piety is really the piety 'of the poor and the simple' (ibid. n. 48). It is the way in which these favourites of the Lord live and express, in their human attitudes and in all the dimensions of life, the mystery of the faith that they have received.

This popular piety, in Mexico and in the whole of Latin America, is indissolubly Marian. In it, Most Holy Mary occupies the same pre-eminent place that she has in Christian faith as a whole. She is the mother, the queen, the protectress and the model. People come to her to honour her, to ask for her intercession, to learn to imitate her, that is, to learn to be real disciples of Jesus. For, as the Lord himself says, 'whoever does the will of God is my brother, and sister, and mother' (Mk. 3:35).

Far from overshadowing the irreplaceable and unique mediation of Christ, this function of Mary, accepted by popular piety, highlights it and 'rather shows its power', as the Second Vatican Council teaches (*Lumen Gentium* n. 60); because everything she is and has 'flows forth from the superabundance of the merits of Christ, rests on his mediation' and leads to him (ibid.). The faithful who come to this sanctuary are well aware of this and put it into practice, always saying with her, looking to God the Father, in the gift of his beloved Son, made present among us by the Spirit: 'My soul magnifies the Lord' (Lk. 1:46).

3. Precisely, when the faithful come to this sanctuary, as I, too, a pilgrim in this Mexican land, wished to come today, what else do they do but praise and honour God the Father, the Son, and the Holy Spirit, in the figure of Mary, who is united by indissoluble ties to the three persons of the Holy Trinity, as the Second Vatican Council also teaches? (cf. *Lumen Gentium* n. 53). Our visit to the Zapopán sanctuary, mine today, yours so many times, signifies in itself the will and the effort to approach God and to let oneself be submerged by him, by means of the intercession, the aid, and the model of Mary.

In these places of grace, so characteristic of the Mexican and Latin American religious area, the People of God, convened in the Church, with its Pastors, and on this happy occasion with the one who humbly presides in the Church over charity (cf. Ignatius of Antioch, *Ad Rom.* prol.), gathers around the altar, under Mary's motherly gaze, to bear witness that what counts in this world and in human life is the opening to the gift of God which is communicated in Jesus, our Saviour, and which comes to us through Mary. It is this that gives our earthly existence its true transcendent dimension, as God willed from the beginning, and as Jesus Christ restored with his death and resurrection, and as shines forth in the Virgin Mary.

She is the refuge of sinners ('refugium peccatorum'). The people of God is aware of its own condition of sin. For this reason, knowing that it needs constant purification, it 'follows constantly the path of penance and renewal' (L.G. n. 8). Each of us is aware of this. Jesus looked for sinners: 'Those who are well have no need of a physician, but those who are sick; I have not come to call the righteous, but sinners to repentance.' (Lk. 5:31–32.) Before curing the man who was paralysed, he said to him: 'Man, your sins are forgiven you.' (Lk. 5:20); and to a woman who had sinned: 'Go, and do not sin again.' (Jn. 8:11.)

If we are oppressed by awareness of sin, we instinctively seek him who has the power to forgive sins (cf. Lk. 5:24), and we seek him through Mary whose sanctuaries are places of conversion, penance, and reconciliation with God.

She awakens in us the hope of mending our ways and persevering in good, even if that may sometimes seem humanly impossible.

She enables us to overcome the multiple 'structures of sin' in which our personal, family, and social life is wrapped. She enables us to obtain the grace of true liberation, with that freedom with which Christ liberated every man.

4. From here starts too, as from its true source, the authentic commitment for other men, our brothers, especially for the poorest and neediest ones, and for the necessary transformation of society. For this is what God wants from us, and it is to this that he sends us, with the voice and the strength of his Gospel, on making us responsible for one another. Mary, as my predecessor Paul VI teaches in the apostolic exhortation *Marialis Cultus* (n. 37), is also a model, the faithful accomplisher of God's will, for those who do not accept passively the adverse circumstances of personal and social life, and are not victims of 'alienation' – as is said today – but who with her proclaim that God is 'the avenger of the humble' and, if necessary, 'puts down the mighty from their thrones', to quote the Magnificat again (cf. Lk. 1:51–53). For, in this way she is 'the type of Christ's perfect disciple who is the architect of the earthly and temporal city, but who, at the same time, aims at the heavenly and eternal city; who promotes justice, liberates the needy, but, above all, bears witness to that active love which constructs Christ in souls' (*Marialis Cultus*, ibid.).

This is Mary Immaculate for us in this sanctuary of Zapopán. This is what we have come to learn from her today, in order that she may always be for these faithful of Guadalajara, for the Mexican nation, and for the whole of Latin America, with its Christian and Catholic being, the real 'star of evangelization'.

5. But I do not want to end this talk without adding some words which I consider important in the context of that which I have just indicated.

This sanctuary of Zapopán, and so many others scattered all over Mexico and Latin-America, where millions of pilgrims come every year with a deep sense of religiousness, can, and must, be privileged places to find an increasingly purified faith which will lead them to Christ.

For this reason, it will be necessary to take great and zealous care over the apostolate in Marian sanctuaries; by means of a suitable and living liturgy; by means of assiduous preaching and sound catechesis; by means of concern for the ministry of the sacrament of Penance; by the prudent purification of any forms of religiousness that present less suitable elements.

It is necessary to take advantage pastorally of these opportunities, sporadic ones, perhaps, of meeting souls that are not always faithful to the whole programme of a Christian life — but who come led by a vision of faith that is sometimes incomplete — in order to try to lead them to the centre of all sound piety, Christ Jesus, the Saviour, Son of God.

In this way popular religiousness will be perfected, when necessary, and Marian devotion will take on its full significance in a trinitarian, Christocentric and ecclesial direction, as the exhortation *Marialis Cultus* so opportunely teaches (n. 25–27).

I call upon the priests in charge of the sanctuaries, and those who guide the pilgrims to them, to reflect carefully on the great good they can do the faithful if they succeed in setting up a suitable system of evangelization.

Do not miss any opportunity to preach Christ, to enlighten the faith of the people and to strengthen it; helping the people on its way towards the Holy Trinity. Let Mary be the way. May Mary Immaculate of Zapopán help you to do so. Amen

WITH THE SEMINARISTS

During the late afternoon, John Paul II
visted the main seminary which was
filled to overflowing with seminarists
from all over Mexico, both diocesan and
religious. His speech to them resembled
a dialogue between the Supreme Pastor
and the aspirants to the ministry of Christ
in the Church:

Dear Seminarians, Diocesan and Religious, of Mexico,

May the peace of the Lord be with you always!

The exuberant and affectionate enthusiasm with which you have received me this afternoon, moves me deeply. I feel an immense joy on sharing with you these moments which confirm beyond any doubt, on your side, the appreciation you feel before God for the Pope; and this instils in me consolation and new courage (cf. 2 Cor. 7:13).

Through you, my inner joy extends to my dear Brothers in the Episcopate, to priests, religious and to all the faithful. Let my deepest gratitude go to all for so many attentions and for such filial cordiality, and even more for remembering me in their prayers to the Lord. I can assure you that your unanimous response to this 'pastoral visit' of mine to Mexico, has given form in me, during these days, to a welcome presentiment. I will express it in the words of the Apostle: 'I rejoice, because I have perfect confidence in you.' (2 Cor. 7:16.)

1. It is a motive of satisfaction for me to know that Mexican seminaries have a long and glorious tradition which goes back to the times of the Council of Trent, with the foundation of the College 'San Pedro' in this city of Guadalajara, in 1570. In the course of time, many other centres of priestly formation, scattered all over the national territory, were added to this one, as a persistent proof of a fresh and vigorous ecclesial vitality. I do not want to pass over in silence the already centenarian Mexican College in Rome. It has a very important mission: to keep alive the bond between Mexico and the Pope's Chair. I consider it the indispensable duty of all to help it and sustain it, so that it can carry out this fundamental task in full faithfulness to the norms of the Magisterium and to the guide-lines given by Peter's See.

This historical concern to create new seminaries arouses in me feelings of satisfaction and approval; but what particularly fills me with hope is the continual flourishing of priestly and religious vocations. I feel happy to see you here, young people overflowing with joy, because you have answered 'yes' to the Lord's invitation to serve him, body and soul, in the Church, in the ministerial priesthood. Like St Paul, I wish to throw my heart wide open to you, to say to you: 'Our heart is wide. . . In return. . . widen your hearts also' (2 Cor. 11–13).

2. Just over two months ago, when I had just begun my Pontificate, I had a eucharistic audience with the seminarians of Rome. As I did then, today I invite you, too, to listen carefully to the Lord who speaks to the heart, especially in prayer and in the liturgy, to discover and to root in the depths of your being the meaning and the value of your vocation.

God who is truth and love, manifested himself to us in the history of creation and in the history of salvation: a history that is still incomplete, that of mankind, which 'waits with eager longing for the revealing of the sons of God' (cf. Rom. 8:18f.). The same God chose us, called us to instil new strength into this history, already knowing that salvation 'is the gift of God, [coming] not because of works, lest any man should boast. For we are his workmanship, created in Christ Jesus' (Eph. 2:8–10). A history, therefore, which is in God's plans, and is also ours, because God wishes us to be workers in the vineyard (cf. Mt. 20:1–16); he wants us to be ambassadors to go and meet everyone and invite everyone to his banquet (ibid. 22:1–14); he wants us to be Good Samaritans who have pity on our unfortunate neighbour (Lk. 10: 30ff.).

3. This would already be enough to see from closer up how great is the vocation. To experience it is a unique event, inexpressible, perceived only as a sweet breath through the awakening touch of grace: a breath of the Spirit who, while he gives a real form to our frail human reality — a clay vessel in the hands of the potter (Rom. 9:20–21) — also lights in our hearts a new light, instils an extraordinary strength which, consolidating us in love, incorporates our existence with the work of God, with his plan of *re-creating* in Christ, that is, the formation of his new redeemed family. You are, therefore, called to construct the church – communion with God – something far above what one can ask or imagine (cf. Eph. 3:14–21).

4. Dear Seminarians, who one day will be ministers of God to plant and water the Lord's field, take advantage of these years in the seminary to fill yourselves with the feelings of Christ himself, in study, prayer, obedience, and the formation of your character. In this way, you will yourselves see how, in proportion as your vocation matures in this school, your life will joyfully assume a specific character, a precise indication: the orientation towards others, like Christ, who 'went about doing good and healing all' (Acts 10:38). In this way, what might seem a misfortune on the human plane, is transformed into a luminous project of life, already examined and approved by Jesus: to live not to be served but to serve (Mt. 20:28).

As you well understand, nothing is further from the vocation than the incentive of earthly advantages, than pursuit of benefits or honours; and the vocation is also very far from being escape from an environment of frustrated hopes or from one which is hostile or alienating. The good news, for him who is called to service of the people of God, in addition to being a call to change and improve one's own existence, is also a call to a life already transformed in Christ, who must be proclaimed and spread.

Let that suffice, dear Seminarians. You will be able to add the rest

yourselves, with your open and generous hearts. I want to add just one thing: love your directors, educators, and superiors. On them there falls the agreeable but difficult task of leading you by the hand along the way that goes to the priesthood. They will help you to acquire a taste for interior life, for the demanding habit of renunciation for Christ, and for disinterestedness; above all, they will infect you with 'the fragrance of the knowledge of Christ' (cf. 2 Cor. 2:14). Do not be afraid. The Lord is with you, and at every moment he is our best guarantee: 'I know whom I have believed.' (2 Tim. 1:12.)

With this trust in the Lord, open your hearts to the action of the Holy Spirit; open them in a resolution of dedication that knows no reservations; open them to the world which is expecting you and needs you; open them to the call already addressed to you by so many souls, to whom, one day, you will be able to give Christ, in the Eucharist, in Penance, in the preaching of the revealed Word, in friendly and disinterested advice, in the serene testimony of your lives as men who are in the world without being of the world.

It is worth dedicating oneself to the cause of Christ, who wants valiant and decided hearts; it is worth devoting oneself to man for Christ, in order to bring him on his way to eternity; it is worth making an option for an ideal that will give you great joys, even if at the same time it demands a good many sacrifices. The Lord does not abandon his followers.

For the Kingdom, it is worth living this precious value of Christianity, priestly celibacy, the centuries-old heritage of the Church; it is worth living it in a responsible way, although it calls for a good many sacrifices. Cultivate devotion to Mary, the Virgin Mother of the Son of God, so that she may help you and urge you to carry it out fully!

But I would also like to reserve a special word for you, educators and superiors of houses of formation to the priesthood. You have a treasure of the Church in your hands. Look after it with the greatest attention and diligence, so that it may produce the hoped-for fruits. Form these young men to wholesome joy, cultivating a rich personality adapted to our time. But form this personality staunch in the faith, in the principles of the Gospel, in awareness of the value of souls, in the spirit of prayer, capable of facing up to the onslaughts of the future.

Do not shorten the vertical view of life, do not lower the exigencies that the option for Christ imposes. If we propose ideals that are distorted, the young will be the first not to want them, because they desire something that is worthwhile, an ideal that is worthy of an existence: although there is a price to pay.

You who are responsible for vocations, priests, religious, fathers and mothers of families, I address these words to you. Commit yourselves generously to the task of procuring new vocations, so important for the future of the Church. The shortage of vocations calls for a responsible effort to remedy it. And this will not be obtained if we are not able to pray, if we are not able to give the vocation to the diocesan or religious priesthood the appreciation and the esteem it deserves.

Young Seminarians! I give all of you my blessing. Christ is waiting for you. You cannot disappoint him.

I have Shared
the Needs of
the Workers

Wednesday 31 January

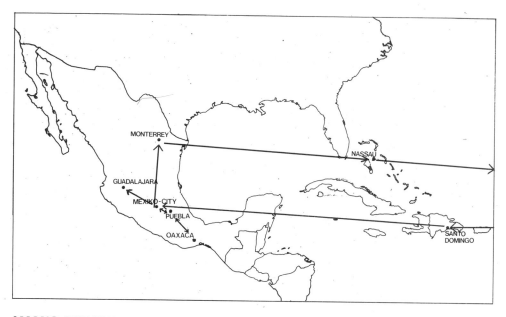

AMONG ONE HUNDRED THOUSAND UNIVERSITY STUDENTS

The Holy Father's day began with Holy Mass which he celebrated at 7 a.m. in the chapel of the Apostolic Delegation, his official residence while in Mexico. Immediately afterwards, John Paul II received, in the Delegation, the Foreign Ministers of Guatemala, Honduras, Nicaragua, Costa Rica and the Minister of Justice of El Salvador. This meeting was not included in the day's programme and it lasted three quarters of an hour. No official communiqué was issued after it.

The first official engagement of the day took place in the square in front of the basilica of Our Lady of Guadalupe where the Pope met a hundred thousand students of Mexico's Catholic Universities and of those of other Latin American countries. The ceremony began at 9.45 a.m. (though fixed for 8 a.m.) with an address by the rector of the La Salle University who assured the Pope of the indefectible commitment of all Catholic Schools for the construction of a better world. A student then spoke, on behalf of all his comrades, and underlined the bond between peace and justice. The Holy Father replied:

Beloved Brothers and Daughters of the Catholic University world,

1. With immense joy and hope I come to this appointment with you, students, professors and lecturers of the Catholic Universities of Mexico, in whom I also see the University world of the whole of Latin America.

Receive my most cordial greeting. It is the greeting of one who feels so much at home among the young, in whom he lays so many hopes; especially when it is a question of such qualified sectors as those that pass through University halls, preparing for a future that will be determinant in society.

Allow me to recall in the first place the members of the Catholic University La Salle, within which this meeting was to have taken place. I recall no less cordially, however, the other Mexican Catholic Universities: the Iberian American University, the Anáhuac University, Monterrey University, the Superior Institute of Educational Sciences in Mexico City, the Faculty of Public Accountancy at Vera Cruz, the Western Institute of Technology and Higher Studies at Guadalajara, Motolinia University, Puebla University for Women, the canonical Faculty of Philosophy in this city, and the Faculty – still in embryo – of Theology, also in this metropolis.

These are young universities. You have, however, a venerable ancestor in the 'Royal and Pontifical University of Mexico', founded on 21 September 1551 with the explicit purpose that in it 'natives and sons of Spaniards should be instructed in matters of the holy Catholic faith and in the other faculties'.

There are also among you – and they are certainly extremely numerous in the whole Mexican territory – Catholic professors and students who teach or study in universities of different denomination. I address my affectionate greeting to them, too, and express my deep joy at knowing that they are all engaged in the same way in establishing the kingdom of Christ.

Let us now extend our view to the vast Latin American horizon. Thus my greeting and thought will dwell with satisfaction on so many other Catholic University Centres, which are a motive of legitimate pride in every nation, where so many enthusiastic looks converge, from whence Christian culture and civilization irradiate. There, persons are formed in the atmosphere of an integral concept of the human being, with scientific precision, and with a Christian view of man, life, society, moral and religious values.

2. And now what more can I say to you in these moments that will necessarily be short? What can the Mexican and Latin American Catholic University world expect from the words of the Pope?

I think I can sum it up, quite synthetically, in three observations, following the line of my venerated predecessor Paul VI.

a) The first one is that the Catholic University must offer a specific contribution to the Church and society, setting itself at a high level of scientific research, deep study of problems and an adequate historical sense.

137

But that is not sufficient for a Catholic University. It must find its ultimate and deep meaning in Christ, in his message of salvation which embraces man in his totality, and in the teaching of the Church.

All this presupposes the promotion of an integral culture, that is, one that aims at the complete development of the human person; one in which emphasis is laid on the values of intelligence, will, conscience, and brotherhood, all of which are based on God the Creator and have been marvellously exalted in Christ (cf. *Gaudium et Spes,* 61): a culture that aims in a disinterested and genuine way at the good of the community and of the whole of society.

b) The second observation is that the Catholic University must form men who are really outstanding for their knowledge, ready to exercise important functions in society and to bear witness to their faith before the world (*Graviss. Educat.* 10). The aim is unquestionably decisive today. Moral and Christian formation must not be considered as something added from outside, but rather as an aspect with which the academic institution is, so to speak, specified and lived. It is a question of promoting and realizing in professors and students a more and more harmonious synthesis between faith and reason, between faith and culture, between faith and life. This synthesis must be obtained not only at the level of research and teaching, but also at the educative-pedagogical level.

c) The third observation is that the Catholic University must be an environment in which Christianity is alive and operating. It is an essential vocation of the Catholic University to bear witness that it is a community seriously and sincerely engaged in scientific research, but also visibly characterized by a real Christian life. That presupposes, among other things, a revision of the figure of the professor, who cannot be considered a mere transmitter of knowledge, but also and above all a witness and educator to true Christian life. In this privileged environment of formation, you, dear students, are called to conscientious and responsible collaboration, free and generous, to realize your formation itself.

3. The establishment of a University apostolate, both as an apostolate of intelligences and as a source of liturgical life, and which must serve the whole University sector of the nation, will not fail to yield precious fruits of human and Christian elevation.

Dear Sons, who dedicate yourselves completely or partially to the Catholic University sector in your respective countries, and all you who, in any University environment, are engaged in establishing the Kingdom of God:

— create a real University family, engaged in the pursuit, which is not always easy, of truth and good, the supreme aspirations of the rational being and the foundations of a solid and responsible moral structure;

— pursue a serious research activity, directing the new generations towards truth, towards human and religious maturity;

— work indefatigably for real and complete progress in your countries.

Without prejudices of any kind, take the hand of those who propose, like you, to construct the real common good;

— unite your forces as bishops, priests, religious men and women, laity, in the planning and implementation of your academic centres and of their activities;

— walk joyfully and tirelessly under the guidance of Holy Mother Church. Her Magisterium, the prolongation of Christ's, is the only guarantee not to stray from the right path, and is a reliable guide to the imperishable inheritance that Christ reserves for those who are faithful to him.

I recommend you all to Eternal Wisdom: 'Wisdom is radiant and unfading, and she is easily discerned by those who love her, and is found by those who seek her.' (Wisdom 6:12.)

May the Seat of Wisdom, which Mexico and the whole of Latin America venerate in Guadalupe Sanctuary, protect you all under her motherly mantle! Amen. And many thanks for your presence.

The Pope then continued with some impromptu remarks and on making a few mistakes in his Spanish, exclaimed 'You see, the Pope too has to go on with his studies.'
The lively meeting came to an end at 10.35 a.m. with the singing by the students and the Pope of Beethoven's 'Hymn to Joy' from the Ninth Symphony.

AT THE FLORIDA COLLEGE
WITH THE JOURNALISTS

John Paul II's next appointment was at
the Florida College with the workers in
the communications media. The Pope
expressed his gratitude to some two
thousand members of the Mexican and
foreign press who had covered his
journeys to Santo Domingo and Mexico.

Dear friends from the world of information,

On many occasions during these days that the enthusiasm of the Mexicans
has made feverish and moving, moments, full of beauty and religious
significance, spent in unforgettable places and environments, I have had the
opportunity to observe you as you went from one place to another, full of
the determination and commitment that distinguishes your task of
information.

I am now on the point of returning to Rome, having attended the
beginning of this important ecclesial event, the Puebla Conference –
marvellous because of its deep significance of unity and creativity for the
future of the Church – and having made a pilgrimage through the
unforgettable lands of the Virgin of Guadalupe. I am grateful to
Providence for granting me at this moment the hoped-for opportunity of
meeting the professionals of information, who have wished to accompany
me on this journey.

Many of you will remain here, to continue to bring the Puebla event to
public opinion, others will accompany me on my return, while still others
will be claimed by further tasks. In any case it is worth taking some
minutes from our crowded timetable to be able to be together, to reflect
and chat a little, this time face to face. For once, we do not have as
intermediary any means of transmission nor do we have the task of making
distant audiences present spiritually. Let us enjoy, without more ado, the
joy of being together.

Of course, I do not forget that behind the cameras there is a person,
that it is a person speaking over the microphone, that it is a person who
corrects and perfects every line of the article that tomorrow's newspaper
will publish. I would like, at this short meeting, to offer my gratitude and
respect to everyone, and address each one by name. I feel the desire and the
necessity to thank each of you for the work of these days, which will
continue in Puebla. It will reflect a Church that welcomes all cultures,
lifestyles, and initiatives, provided they aim at the construction of the
kingdom of God.

I understand the tensions and difficulties in which your work takes
place. I am well aware of the effort that the communication of news
requires. I can imagine the labour involved in transferring all this
complicated equipment of yours from one place to another, putting it up

and taking it down. I also realize that your work calls for long journeys, and separates you from your family and friends. It is not an easy life, but, in return, like all creative activities, especially those that signify a service for others, it is particularly rewarding. I am sure that you all have experience of this.

I remember now a similar occasion, a few weeks ago, when I had the opportunity to chat with the professionals who had come to give information on my election and on the inauguration of the Pontificate. I referred to this profession as a vocation. One of the most important documents of the Church, that on social communications, declares that 'modern man cannot do without information that is full, consistent, accurate and true' (*Communio et Progressio,* 34); and it proclaims that when such information is furnished through the media of social communication, it makes 'every man a partner in the business of the human race' (*C.P.* 19).

With your talent and experience, your professional competence, the necessary inclination and the means at your disposal, you can facilitate this great service for humanity. And, above all, like the best of yourselves, you wish to be seekers of truth, to offer it to all those who wish to hear it. First of all, serve truth, that which is constructive, that which improves and dignifies man.

To the extent to which you pursue this ideal, I assure you that the Church will remain at your side, because this is also her ideal. She loves truth and freedom: freedom to know the truth, to preach it and to communicate it to others.

The time has come to say goodbye and to express to you again my gratitude for the service rendered to the diffusion of the truth which is manifested in Christ, and which is being expressed in these days in acts of utmost importance for the life of faith in these American countries, so close to the Church. We take leave of each other with respect and friendship, ready to be consistent with our best ideals. The Pope is happy to greet you and bless you — remembering the media you represent: newspapers, television networks, broadcasting stations — and also your families. I frequently offer my prayer for you yourselves and for them. May the Lord accompany you.

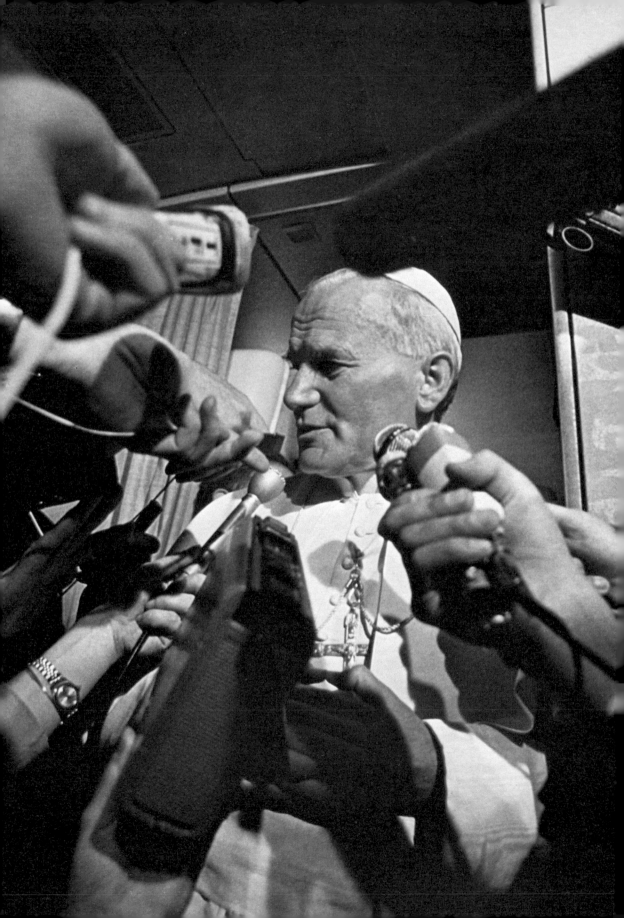

THE RODEO OF THE CHARROS

The last of the Pope's engagements in Mexico City was in the form of recreation. At a ranch not far from the capital, John Paul II watched an exhibition of their skills by the *charros,* Mexico's cowboys, organized in his honour by the association of the *Charros del Pedregal.* After a speech of welcome by the chaplain of the association, Padre Roberto Gonzalez, these fearless riders gave a dazzling display of their dexterity in horseback riding and lassoing. When they had finished, the Pope thanked them for a wonderful show which was an eloquent expression of their spirit and culture. He then blessed the *charros.*

THE DEPARTURE FROM MEXICO CITY

The Pope returned to the Apostolic Delegation towards 1 p.m. only to leave again an hour later for the airport where a DC10 was waiting to fly him to Monterrey. This was the Pope's farewell to Mexico City and the inhabitants turned out in swarms to see him off. Millions of people formed a thick barrier on either side of the ten kilometre route which leads from the Apostolic Delegation to the airport. A hail of multi-coloured confetti and of yellow and white carnations poured down on the cortège from windows and balconies. The irrepressible enthusiasm of the crowds delayed the arrival at the airport, adding to the delays already accumulated during the morning. After blessing the tens of thousands of people there present and exchanging brief farewells with the Archbishop, Monsignor Ernesto Corripio Ahumado, and with the civic authorities, the Pope boarded his aircraft at 3.40 p.m. Immediately after take-off, the Mexican Airlines DC10 slowly circled twice over the capital while, on the ground, hundreds of thousands of people provided with small mirrors flashed back the sun's rays in the direction of the plane.

AT MONTERREY

The aeroplane reached its destination at about 5.10 p.m., two hours after the scheduled time. Monterrey is the capital of the northern state of León, the third largest city in Mexico and the first in economic importance thanks to its many steel, machine tool, textile and chemical industries. The whole city, which is predominantly working class, turned out to welcome the Pope. Enormous crowds, waving Mexican and Vatican flags, assembled at the airport and along the esplanade of the Rio Santa Caterina to which the Pope was carried by helicopter. 'Poland, Poland' and 'The Worker Pope' and 'Christ the Worker' were the cries most frequently heard among the crowd.

On his arrival at the main square, often interrupted by ovations from the throng, the Pope heard an address of welcome from the Metropolitan Archbishop, Monsignor Jos del Jesus Tirado Pedraza, who laid stress on the two main characteristics of the people of Monterrey, their religious fervour and their capacity for work.

After a further speech by a working man, the Pope replied as follows:

Peasants, Clerks and, above all, Workers of Monterrey,

Thank you for all that I have been able to hear. Thank you for all that I can see. Many thanks to one and all.

I thank you heartily for this warm and cordial welcome to your industrial city of Monterrey. Your existence revolves around it, and your daily work to earn a living for yourselves and for your children takes place in it. It is also a witness to your sorrows and to your aspirations. It is your work, the work of your hands and your intelligence; and in this sense it is a symbol of your pride as workers, and a sign of hope for new progress and for an increasingly human life.

I am happy to be among you as your friend and brother, as a fellow worker in this city of Monterrey, which is for Mexico something similar to what Nueva Hutta means in my distant and beloved Krakow. I do not forget the difficult years of the World War in which I myself had direct experience of physical work such as yours, of daily toil and its dependence, its heaviness and monotony. I shared the necessities of the workers, their rightful demands and their legitimate aspirations. I know very well the need that work should not alienate and frustrate, but should correspond to man's higher dignity.

146

I can testify to one thing: in the most difficult moments, the Polish people found in their faith in God, in their confidence in the Blessed Virgin, the Mother of God, in the ecclesial community united around its pastors, a light greater than the darkness, and an unshakeable hope. I know that I am speaking to workers who are aware of their state as Christians, and who want to live this state with all its dynamism and consequences.

For this reason, the Pope wishes to make some reflections to you which concern your dignity as men and as sons of God. From this double source will spring the light to give shape to your personal and social existence. In fact, if the spirit of Jesus Christ dwells in us, we must feel priority concern for those who do not have enough food, clothes, housing, and those who do not have access to cultural goods. Since work is the source of one's livelihood, collaboration with God in improving nature, a service for brothers which ennobles man, Christians cannot fail to take an interest in the problem of the unemployment of so many men and women, above all, young people and heads of households, whom unemployment leads to discouragement and despair.

Those who have the fortune to work, wish to do so in more human and secure conditions, to participate more justly in the fruit of the common effort as regards wages, social insurances, and the possibilities of cultural and spiritual development. They want to be treated as free and responsible men, called to take part in the decisions that concern their lives and their future. It is their fundamental right freely to create organizations to defend and promote their own interests and to contribute responsibly to the common good. The task is an immense and complex one. It is complicated today by the world economic crisis, the disorder of unjust commercial and financial circles, the rapid exhaustion of some resources, and the risks of irreversible contamination of the biophysical environment.

To take a real part in the united effort of humanity, the Latin American peoples rightly demand that there should be returned to them their rightful responsibility over the goods that nature has bestowed on them, and general conditions that will enable them to carry out a development in conformity with their own spirit, with the participation of all the human groups that make them up. Bold and renewing innovations are necessary in order to overcome the serious injustices inherited from the past and to meet the challenge of the prodigious transformations of mankind.

The new realities call for new attitudes at all levels, national and international, and on the part of all social groups and of all systems. Unilateral denunciation of the other and the easy pretext of alien ideologies, whatever they may be, are more and more ridiculous excuses.

If mankind wishes to control an evolution that is slipping from its hand, if it wants to avoid the materialistic temptation that is gaining ground in a desperate flight forwards, if it wants to ensure true development for men and for peoples, it must radically revise the concepts of progress which, under different names, have let spiritual values waste away.

The Church offers her aid. She does not fear forceful denunciation or attacks on human dignity. But she keeps her essential energies to help men and human groups, contractors and workers, in order that they may become aware of the immense reserves of goodness they have within them, which they have already caused to yield fruit in their history, and which must give new fruit today.

The working-class movement, to which the Church and Christians have made an original and different contribution, particularly in this continent, claims its rightful share of responsibility in the construction of a new world order. It has gathered the common aspirations of freedom and dignity. It has developed the values of solidarity, brotherhood and friendship. In the experience of sharing, it has brought forth original forms of organizations, improving substantially the fate of many workers, and contributing, although people do not always want to admit this, to making a mark in the industrial world. Relying on this past, it will have to commit itself to looking for new ways, it will have to renew itself and contribute even more decisively to constructing the Latin America of the future.

It is ten years since my predecessor Paul VI went to Colombia. He wished to bring to the peoples of Latin America the consolation of the Common Father. He wished to open to the Universal Church the riches of the Churches of this continent. Some years afterwards, celebrating the eightieth anniversary of the first social encyclical, *Rerum Novarum*, he wrote: 'The social teaching of the Church, with all its dynamism, accompanies men in their quest. Even if it does not intervene to give authenticity to a determined structure or to propose a prefabricated model, it does not confine itself just to recalling some general principles. It evolves by means of a reflection that matures in contact with the changing situations of this world, under the impetus of the Gospel as a source of renewal, since its message is accepted in its totality and in its requirements. It develops with the sensitivity characteristic of the Church, marked by a disinterested will for service and attention to the poorest. It is nourished, finally, by a rich experience of many centuries, which enables it to assume in the continuity of its permanent concerns the bold creating innovation that the present situation of the world requires.' They are words of Paul VI.

Dear Friends: in obedience to these principles the Church wishes to draw attention today to a serious phenomenon that is very topical: the problem of migrants. We cannot close our eyes to the situation of millions of men who, in their search for work and for livelihood have to leave their country and often their family. They have to cope with the difficulties of a new environment that is not always pleasant and welcoming, an unknown language, and general conditions that plunge them into solitude and, sometimes, social exclusion for themselves and for their wives and children; even when advantage is not taken of these circumstances to offer lower wages, to reduce social insurance and welfare benefits, and to give housing conditions unworthy of a human being. There are occasions on which the principle put into practice is that of obtaining the maximum performance from the emigrant worker without looking to the person. Faced with this phenomenon, the Church continues to proclaim that the principle to follow in this, as in other fields, is not that of allowing economic, social, and political factors to prevail over man, but, on the contrary, for the dignity of the human person to be put above everything else, and for the rest to be conditioned by it.

We would create a world unpleasant to live in if we aimed only at having more, and did not think first and foremost of the person of the worker, his conditions as a human being and a son of God who is called to an eternal vocation, if we did not think of helping him to be more.

Certainly, on the other side, the worker has obligations to carry out loyally, since otherwise there cannot be a just social order.

I make a forceful appeal to the public authorities, contractors and workers, to reflect on these principles and to deduce the consequent lines of action. It must also be recognized that there is no lack of examples of those who put into practice, in an exemplary way, these principles of the social doctrine of the Church. I rejoice at this. I praise those in charge, and encourage others to imitate their example. This will be to the advantage of the cause of harmony and brotherhood among social groups and nations. It will be to the advantage even of the economy. Above all, it will be to the advantage of the cause of humanity.

But let us not stop just a man. The Pope brings you yet another message. It is a message for you, workers of Mexico and Latin America: Open up to God. God loves you. Christ loves you. The Mother of God, the Virgin Mary, loves you. The Church and the Pope love you and call upon you to follow the irresistible force of love, which can overcome everything and can build-up. When nearly two thousand years ago God sent us his Son, he did not wait until human efforts had eliminated all types of injustice. Jesus Christ came to share our human condition, with its suffering, its difficulties, its death. Before transforming daily existence, he managed to speak to the hearts of the poor, to free them from sin, to open their eyes to a horizon of light and to fill them with joy and hope. Jesus Christ, who is present in your churches, in your families, in your hearts, in your entire lives, does the same today. Open all doors to him. Let us all, united in these moments, joyfully celebrate the love of Jesus and his Mother. Let no one feel excluded, in particular the most underprivileged, since this joy comes from Jesus Christ and is not offensive for any sorrow. It has the savour and the warmth of the friendship offered to us by him who suffered more than we, who died on the cross for us, who prepares an eternal dwelling for us by his side, and who already in this life proclaims and affirms our dignity as men, as sons of God.

I am with worker friends and I would like to stay with you far longer. But I must conclude. To you present here, to your companions in Mexico, and to all your fellow-countrymen working outside their native country, to all the workers of Latin America, I leave my greeting as a friend, my blessing and my memory.

My brotherly embrace for all of you, for your children and the members of your family.

At the end of this brief but stirring
encounter with the workers of Monterrey,
the Pope blessed the people of the city
and then returned to the airport by
helicopter.

A HALT AT NASSAU

The same evening, the Pope's plane took
off for Nassau in the Bahamas where it
landed during the night for a routine
check before proceeding on its
trans-Atlantic flight. A big crowd had
joined the principal authorities at the
airport to welcome the Holy Father. The
honours of the occasion were carried out
in the Queen Elizabeth Stadium where
the Pope thanked both the population
and the authorities for their warm
welcome and extended his best wishes
for the peace and progress of this young
country in the new world:

I am grateful to you for this welcome. It is a great joy for me, on my
return to Rome, to be able to stop in Nassau — a great joy to be with the
beloved people of the Bahamas.

My first greeting goes to the authorities of this young, recently
independent nation. You have kindly facilitated my visit, and I wish to
assure you of my cordial gratitude. You have, moreover, my prayers for the
faithful fulfilment of the lofty tasks that you are called to perform at the
service of all the men and women of this nation.

Being here this evening in your midst, I have the opportunity to
formulate my best wishes for the entire population of the Bahamas. My
hope for everyone is that there may be constant progress along the path of
authentic and integral human advancement. With the profound conviction
of the surpassing dignity of the human person, may all the people of these
islands make their individual and unique contributions to the common
good of all — a common good that takes into account the personal rights
and duties of all citizens.

To be with you is also to share the hope that, as a sovereign nation
within the family of nations, you will make your own special contribution
to society: that you will help build the edifice of world peace on the solid
columns of truth and justice, charity and freedom. And may God bless all
your efforts and help you to fulfil this important role for the benefit of this
generation and of those to come.

On this wonderful occasion I wish to extend a particular word of
greeting to all the sons and daughters of the Catholic Church. I assure you
all of my love in our Lord Jesus Christ, and I trust that my presence is a
real indication to you of the great bonds of faith and charity that link you
with Catholics everywhere throughout the world. I pray that you will find
strength and joy in this solidarity and fellowship, and that you will
constantly give witness to your belief by the genuineness of your Christian
lives. The words of Jesus constitute a perpetual challenge for all of us: 'Let
your light so shine before men, that they may see your good works and
give glory to your Father who is in heaven' (Mt. 5:16).

With deep respect and fraternal love I wish also to greet all the other Christian brethren of the Bahamas — all who confess with us that 'Jesus Christ is the Son of God' (1 Jn. 4:15). Be assured of our desire to collaborate loyally and perseveringly, in order to attain by God's grace the unity willed by Christ the Lord. My expression of friendship goes likewise to all the men and women of good will residing in this region of the

Atlantic ocean. As children of one heavenly Father we are united in the solidarity of love and in promoting to the full the incomparable dignity of the human person.

At this moment then, during this short stop, I sense the hope that is in all of you, the people of the Bahamas — a hope for your future that is vast like the ocean that surrounds you. It is my privilege to share this hope with you and to give expression to it now, being confident that it will sustain you in all your worthy endeavours as a united people. I ask God to lead you to the full achievement of your destiny. May he give to the people of the Bahamas rich and lasting blessings. May he assist the poor, comfort the sick, guide the youth, and bring peace to every heart.

God bless the Bahamas, today and for ever!

At 1.30 a.m. the Pope's plane resumed its
flight towards Italy.

THE ARRIVAL AT ROME AIRPORT

No sooner had he left the aircraft, which had brought him back to Rome, than John Paul II walked across to a dais on which microphones were set up. After listening to a tribute from the Prime Minister of Italy, Signor Andreotti, representing the Italian Government, the Holy Father said:

I was very happy, Mr Prime Minister, to hear the courteous words of greeting and good wishes that you kindly addressed to me, also on behalf of the Italian Government.

At the end of this first apostolic journey, which took me over the Ocean to the noble and dear land of Mexico, one feeling prevails over the others that fill my anxious and stirred heart: the feeling of gratitude.

I am grateful, in the first place, to the Lord and to the Holy Virgin of Guadalupe for the constant assistance with which they sustained me in these days; allowing me to crown happily a delicate and important initiative, undertaken in fulfilment of the universal mandate which Christ himself entrusted to me, calling me to the responsibility of his Vicar in Peter's See.

I think next, with deep gratitude, of the many demonstrations of thoughtfulness, devotedness, and affection, on the part of the people that I met in the course of my pilgrimage; and, in particular, on the part of my revered brothers in the Episcopate, gathered in Puebla in representation of the whole Catholic Hierarchy of Latin America. My heart was able to beat in unison with theirs: I rejoiced, suffered and hoped with them; above all, I prayed with them, imploring from our common Father the advent of a world made more peaceful, just, and human by sincere adherence to the message of love of his Son incarnate.

And now, on my return to this Roman See, in which the Catholic world recognizes the centre and the source of its own unity, a new and great emotion is aroused in me by this welcome of yours, so spontaneous and cordial. I greet, therefore, with respect and gratitude, the Cardinal Secretary of State and the other ecclesiastical personalities, the Italian political, civil, and military Authorities, the members of the Diplomatic Corps, and all of you who have disregarded inconvenience in order to be able to welcome me personally.

May God reward you for such courtesy, and may he lavish his favours on you and on all those who have made every possible effort to ensure the success of the journey; beginning with the executives, pilots and personnel of the Air Companies, to whom I owe an agreeable and comfortable flight. In confirmation of these wishes I am happy to impart to you present here, to the beloved city of Rome, and to all those who followed me in thought and in prayer, a special comforting Apostolic Blessing.

THE RETURN TO THE VATICAN

On his return to the Vatican, Pope John Paul II was received in the Hall of the Consistory by the Cardinals present in Rome who congratulated him warmly on the great success he had achieved in Latin America. After hearing a speech of homage by the Dean of the Sacred College, Cardinal Carlo Confalonieri, the Pope spoke as follows:

Lords Cardinals,

1. At the moment when my first missionary journey ends, I raise my deepest thanks to God for the great experience he has granted me of living in the fullness of an apostolic work which occupied, with particular intensity, every hour of the past days.

2. I considered it my duty to undertake this journey (connected with the work of the third General Assembly of the Latin American Episcopate in Puebla, announced some time ago), following, in this, the example of my predeccesor Paul VI of venerated memory, who wished to inaugurate this new form in carrying out the papal office in the Church.

3. It is difficult to speak fully of this unforgettable experience while the thousand voices I listened to still re-echo in my mind, and while the memories of what I was able to see, of the persons that I was able to meet, and of the subjects I had occasion to tackle, are still so immediate and alive.

4. It will be necessary to return to all that for a long time in prayer, reflection, and in my heart. But I can say right now that this journey, after the short but significant stop at Santo Domingo, was an exceptional meeting with Mexico in its human and Christian reality, a meeting with the people of God of this country, which responded with a great act of faith to the presence of the Pope. This meeting, which started in Guadalupe, the heart of the Mexican Church, extended to reach the stages of Puebla in Oaxaca, Guadalajara, and Monterrey.

5. With the riches of its contents and the multiplicity of its manifestations, this meeting offers, in a certain sense, a living context for the tasks which, together with the Bishops of Latin America, we tackled within the third General Assembly of that episcopate. The latter, which, as you know, opened on 27 January last with the solemn concelebration at the Sanctuary of the Virgin of Guadalupe, continues at Puebla, on the subject 'Evangelization in the present and future of Latin America,' until 12 February next, when it concludes.

Introducing its work on 28 January, I addressed to the South American Church, with great hope and confidence, a message which was made concretely universal by the presence of the media of social communications, and by that of the professionals of information (who gave great coverage to every stage of my short but intense journey).

It will certainly be necessary to speak more than once of the significance of the work of Puebla and of the individual problems tackled there, examining the various subjects again.

6. Now, returning to the Apostolic See after seven days, I feel the need to thank heartily all those, at every level, who helped to prepare and organize this journey. It has been a great success, although it took place in such a short time.

I would like to thank also all those who bore with me the weight of this journey: Their Excellencies Caprio, Casaroli, Martin, Marcinkus, Mons, Noè, and all the other persons of the suite, press, radio and television, and all the lay people who followed me throughout the whole journey.

7. Finally, for the welcome you have given me, allow me to express my thanks particularly to you and to the whole College of Cardinals, whom I felt so close in prayer and in their hearts in the course of these unforgettable days; especially to the Cardinal Dean who has interpreted so well the sentiments of you all, and to the Cardinal Secretary of State for the precious work he carried out so generously in the days of my absence.

May the Virgin of Guadalupe, to whom I have prayed so much in these days, through her intercession, give strength to our commitment in order that the hopes raised by the apostolic journey that I have concluded today, will not be disappointed.